HISTORICAL RECORD
OF THE
BRITISH LEGION SCOTLAND

"WE WILL REMEMBER"

Historical Record

of the

British Legion Scotland

by

LT. COL. GEORGE MALCOLM OF POLTALLOCH

Published by

THE BRITISH LEGION SCOTLAND

EDINBURGH

ACKNOWLEDGMENTS

IT is difficult in a small space to enumerate all who have supplied material and assisted in research to enable this volume to be written, but most grateful thanks are expressed to all British Legion Scotland office-bearers, members and officials including those of the Women's Section, for their valuable help.

No list of acknowledgments would be complete without a reference to our advertisers who, by kindly taking space, have gone a long way to assist on the publication side. In addition to those whose advertisements actually appear, generous donations towards the cost of publication have been received from : The Culter Mills Paper Co. Ltd., Aberdeenshire ; The Dunlop Rubber Co. (Scotland) Ltd., Glasgow ; Jenners Ltd., Edinburgh ; McCorquodale & Co. Ltd., London ; Wm. Teacher & Sons Ltd., Glasgow ; The Reid Gear Co. Ltd., Paisley ; and Rolls Royce Ltd., Derby.

We also have to thank the Press of Scotland and others, and Dorothy Wilding Portraits Ltd. (colour portrait of H.M. The Queen) for kindly allowing us to reproduce photographs without fee.

D.M.

First Published 1959

Printed in Edinburgh
By McLAGAN & CUMMING LTD.

CONTENTS

ROYAL PATRONS, BRITISH LEGION SCOTLAND,
PAST AND PRESENT

H.R.H. THE PRINCE OF WALES
(later H.M. KING EDWARD VIII, now H.R.H. THE DUKE OF WINDSOR)

HIS LATE MAJESTY KING GEORGE VI

HER MAJESTY THE QUEEN

ROYAL GRAND PRESIDENT, WOMEN'S SECTION,
BRITISH LEGION SCOTLAND

H.M. QUEEN ELIZABETH, THE QUEEN MOTHER

H.M. The Queen

Royal Patron, British Legion Scotland

CHAPTER I

BIRTH OF A MOVEMENT

" I have done the State some service "

WHEN, after nearly five years, the guns ceased their thundering on 11th November 1918, the non-professional element in the greatest British Army ever known began to look over its shoulder and to wonder whether and how soon it would be possible to resume normal life and occupation. These gallant men had left their own interests behind them when they put on the King's uniform for an indefinite period, and they nursed a real and justifiable foreboding that homes and employment were likely to be more than a little difficult to obtain in competition with their more fortunate friends in exempted occupations at home. As for those whom wounds and sickness had wholly or partially incapacitated, what chance would they stand in the post-war labour market? True, if they had been lucky enough to belong to a Regiment with a well-run Old Comrades Association, they could expect a little help from that quarter ; but these Associations were neither financially nor administratively geared to deal with such a volume of cases as the war had produced. Something more powerful, and more universal, was needed to grapple with the multiplicity of problems confronting the four million soldiers returning to civilian life in a grateful, but disorganised, country. And while many were fortunate in being welcomed back to work by their former employers, many more were facing starvation and ruin with their families. Unemployment caused homes to be sold up, and misery was widespread throughout the ranks of the returned " heroes." (For so they were named in a current political phrase which spoke of making Great Britain " a land fit for heroes to live in." A well-known comedian went nearer the truth when he sang " You have to *be* a hero to live in it at all ! ")

Fortunately, among those who had early been restored to civil life were some with sufficient foresight to realize the full portent of these things, and to appreciate at their real worth the promises that had been made on the recruiting platform—promises that ample provision would be made for the widow and dependent ; that legislation would be passed providing for adequate pensions and comfort for the maimed ; and that suitable housing would be found for all. Their aim, in general terms, was not only to perpetuate the memory of the fallen, but to obtain justice for those who had suffered, and to accomplish this by guarding and developing their great spirit of comradeship which had animated all ranks of the Army in the Field.

To this end there had been formed ex-Service Associations of various kinds, of which four stood out as most powerful, with branches all over the country. These were :—

1. The National *Federation* of Discharged and Demobilized Sailors and Soldiers.
2. The National *Association* of Discharged Sailors and Soldiers.
3. The Comrades of the Great War.
4. The Officers' Association.

Photograph by courtesy of " Edinburgh Evening News."

The Royal Scots Greys leading the Royal Procession of the 1953 State Visit of Her Majesty The Queen. The British Legion Scotland lined the route outside Princes Street Station. (From *The Claymore*, September 1953.)

H.M. The Queen Mother, when Queen, inspecting the Parade of members of the Newburgh Branch during her tour of the Fife Boroughs. (From *The Claymore*, January 1951.)

All these Associations were independent of each other, and therefore lacked cohesion ; and if the First World War taught us one thing above all others, it was the paramount importance of unity of command and unity of purpose in achieving the desired end. Consequently, there was little result attained by their disjointed efforts. Moreover, in the uncertain state of national affairs at that time there existed a considerable danger that these, and similar powerful organizations, might be tempted to play an important part in politics and seek by political pressure to obtain their ends. The National Federation had in fact assumed a definitely left wing outlook, and refused to admit officers to membership. The Comrades, on the other hand, displayed a predominately conservative bias. In England this diversion of views had led to physical clashes in various places, and it was generally realised that these warring bodies of ex-Servicemen must be persuaded to unite if any progress was ever to be made. The one man capable of effecting this unification, as all were agreed, was Field-Marshal Earl Haig, who had led them united to the final victory in France. He himself, fully aware of what was needed, had already while Commander-in-Chief Home Forces, collaborated with Sir Frederick Maurice in the formation of the Officers' Association, which they had determined should be free of any political complexion, and thus serve as an intermediary to bring the Federation and the Comrades together. In advance of the general feeling, Lord Haig had been for two years (in the words of Sir Ian Hamilton) " stumping the country in Scotland " trying to raise money for the officers, for the wounded, for the widows and orphans, and unconsciously paving the way for the Legion. Such was the respect and sympathy that he created both for himself as a man and a leader, and for the very necessary work which he was undertaking, that the difficulties of persuading the leaders of these four Associations to amalgamate under his leadership were minimised and overcome, and that by June 1921, at a Meeting in the Usher Hall, Edinburgh, the British Legion (Scotland) had been formed. It is not too much to say that without his strong character and personality this great Scottish institution (for such it is) would not have come into being for several years, to the grave detriment of ex-Servicemen as a community. And so it was that this magnanimous soldier, who might well have wished (and would certainly have been entitled) to spend the years of peace in enjoyment of the honours and the leisure which he had so well earned, chose instead to devote himself heart and soul to the cause of those who had helped him rise to fame. Unity, Comradeship and Peace were his watchwords : Unity between all ex-Servicemen working in a spirit of Comradeship, and maintaining Peace, not only within their own ranks, but in the community at large.

His biographer, the late Lord Norwich, comments on his views as to the way in which the Legion should be controlled and administered :—

" *It is interesting to note that he never attempted, as he might easily have done, to assume dictatorial powers in a position where they would probably have been gladly accorded to him. It would not have been surprising if one whose whole career and whole outlook had been so strictly military had allowed something of the regimental tradition to creep into the control and discipline of this new body of which he was the head. But, on the contrary, he was not only anxious that in the Legion the old hierarchy should be forgotten, but that the Constitution should be as democratic as that of any other body of free men who associate together for purposes of mutual advantage. Having, however, secured his first objective of bringing ex-officers and men*

4

into the same organization, he realised that, if steps were not taken to prevent it, the control of the different branches and of the organization itself was likely to drift into the hands of those who had held commissions. Therefore to ignore the previous position of men who joined the Legion, which on the face of it appeared the more democratic method, would, in practice, probably defeat the very end that it had in view.

" ' Really,' he wrote to Colonel Crosfield on 14th March 1922, ' there ought to be no question of rank in the Legion—we are all Comrades. That, however, is not possible, and so we must legislate to ensure that the other ranks are adequately represented.' "

The first Unity Conference (significant title, for how seldom do Scotsmen agree to sink their differences) was held in Edinburgh on 18th June 1921. Colonel Sir William Dick-Cunyngham, Bart., from the chair, put his finger on the point in his opening remarks when he said

" There had never been a better opportunity for those who desire the well-being of ex-Servicemen than at present. In the past there was never a proper co-ordination to enable one organization to approach the Government with a united demand from the ex-servicemen,"

and he hoped this would be different in the future.

The first concrete act of the Conference was to adopt, unanimously, the title of " The British Legion." (This was amended in August to read " The British Legion (Scotland) " ; but it was not until 1950 that the brackets were removed from the word Scotland.) The next thing achieved was the adoption of two important Resolutions, the first of which established the National Executive Council ; and the second underlined the strong desire for World Peace which animated every soldier who had fought on either side in the 1914-1918 War. They are quoted in full here below :—

1. " That this Conference constitutes the Provisional Unity Committee consisting of four representatives of the Officers' Association, the Scottish Federation of ex-Servicemen, the Comrades of the Great War, and the National Association of Discharged Sailors and Soldiers, to be the first Executive Council of the British Legion, and that the period of office of the said Council be limited to May 1922 ; and prior to that time the Council take the necessary action to ensure the election of the Scottish Executive Council in accordance with the Constitution.

2. " That this Conference of the United Organization of ex-Service officers and men having in view the great power for Peace which can be exerted by the co-operation of ex-Servicemen's organizations in Entente Countries, instructs the Council to affiliate at once with the Inter-Allied Federation of ex-Servicemen."

Once formed, the Executive Council lost no time in setting itself up as a working body, and held its first meeting at 28 Rutland Square, Edinburgh (the National Headquarters) on 20th August 1921. One of its original decisions had been that the whole Legion's affairs should be centred in Edinburgh, and so, although from time to time the address of Headquarters was changed, the offices always remained in Edinburgh. The present site, Haig House, is admirable in that it also accommodates the offices of other ex-Service Associations which all work in conjunction with the Legion.

5

So many famous products come in U.G.B. bottles

So MANY of the good things you buy come in U.G.B. containers — and are all the better for it. Foods and drinks. Toiletries, cosmetics, medicines, cleaners and polishes. All of them reach you in tip-top condition — at their best and looking their best — in U.G.B. bottles and jars.

U.G.B. specialise in making the right container for every kind of product — and making it really well.

United Glass
Bottle Manufacturers Ltd.

Britain's most experienced glass container manufacturers

53 Bothwell Street, Glasgow, C.2   Tel: Central 5946

One of the first steps in organizing the Legion throughout the country was to divide Scotland into seven geographical Areas,[1] with active " Councils " in each who, it was hoped, would bring the existing ex-Servicemen's clubs and branches within the orbit of the Legion. This proved, in some Areas, more difficult than had been anticipated owing, largely, to local jealousies ; but Kilmarnock (later Ayrshire) Area showed the way by inducing their six Comrades branches to accept membership of the Legion as early as 1921. Others were not so fortunate in their endeavours, and although there were 23 branches by 1924, the majority seem to have been formed somewhere between 1926 and 1932.

A Constitution was drawn up which may fairly be said to have stood the test of time. Although detailed amendments have been adopted by the Annual Conference from time to time, the Principles and Policy and the Aims and Objects of the Constitution have remained unaltered in scope. A summary of this basically important document in relation to the working of the Legion is given in Appendix A.

From its inception the Legion has enjoyed Royal Patronage, for its first Patron was H.R.H. The Prince of Wales, who had himself won the M.C. while serving with the Grenadier Guards in the line. He was followed by his brother, King George VI, who had served at sea in the Battle of Jutland, and on his death in 1952 his daughter, our present Queen (who has carried out her National Service in the A.T.S.) became Patron. The following year her husband, Prince Philip (who had served in the Royal Navy both during and after the War) was specially elected as an ordinary member, without subscription, by the Annual Conference. Royalty, until 1939, had also graciously attended Remembrance Day Services in Edinburgh.

Thus, firmly established and recognized at the start, the Executive Committee set about the gigantic task of fulfilling the aims and objects as defined in Rule 3 of its adopted Constitution. These are many and various and are given in full in Appendix A. It is sufficient here to say that these public-spirited gentlemen who formed that first Executive Committee, and their successors to-day, shirked nothing in their conscientious pursuit of these aims ; and by their steadfast endeavours, voluntarily undertaken, proved themselves the living embodiment of the Legion's Motto—" Service, Not Self ! "

A General Secretary, Mr Baxter, with an assistant, Mr Johnstone, were appointed ; and the work went forward so well that by June 1922, when the next Annual Conference took place, the Executive Council was able to report the following tangible results achieved between January and May that year :—

7,645 cases taken up in respect of Pensions, Medical Claims, Arrears of Pay, etc.

246 Appellants had been represented at the Pensions Appeal Tribunal.

The sum of £3,546, 14s. 3d. had been recovered.

Such was the beginning of the work which grew to such enormous dimensions in the tide of the First World War, subsided slightly, and then

---

[1] The original Areas were called Aberdeen, Kilmarnock, Dundee, Glasgow, Fife and Kinross, Edinburgh and Inverness. These have now been increased to nine. For details see Appendix E.

Whether you live in Edinburgh or Glasgow

you are within easy reach of R. W. Forsyth's, famous for quality, service and reliability. There, your every purchase—be it tailoring, outfitting, footwear, or sports equipment— is certain to give you complete and lasting satisfaction.

. . . And if you have the impression that quality is beyond the reach of people of modest means, you are in for a pleasant surprise here.

R. W. FORSYTH

Renfield Street Glasgow   R. W. Forsyth Ltd   Princes Street Edinburgh

swelled up again in the aftermath of a Second World War—work which cannot, even after fifteen years of Peace, be called finished.

If the great Field-Marshal, the Founder, could see his Legion as it lives to-day, he might justly say (with more modesty than Othello)

" I have done the State some service "

Coated Papers
for every purpose

Apart from White Art Papers we specialise in
Colours of Great Variety

Samuel Jones & Co.
(Devonvale) Ltd.

DEVONVALE MILLS
TILLICOULTRY   SCOTLAND

Telephone: *Telegrams:*
TILLICOULTRY 242 (four lines)   " JONES, TILLICOULTRY "

Sales Offices for England: *Export Sales Office:*
SAMUEL JONES & CO. LTD.   SAMUEL JONES & CO. (EXPORT) LTD.
16-17 New Bridge Street   16-17 New Bridge Street
London, E.C.4   London, E.C.4

CHAPTER II

BETWEEN THE WARS

"And everybody praised the Duke
Who this great fight did win,
'But what good came of it at last?'
Quoth little Peterkin
'Why that I cannot tell,' said he,
'But 'twas a famous victory.'"

IT is said that a lady once observed to the great Duke of Wellington that he must have been proud to have won such a great victory as Waterloo. To which the Duke is said to have replied " Madam, there is no greater disaster than a great Victory—unless it be a great Defeat." The result of this apparent paradox was well known to Field-Marshal Lord Haig, and it was to combat the dangers of indolence on the one hand and political strife on the other that he strove so valiantly for the British Legion and its self-declared aim of Comradeship.

He was the first and obvious choice for National President ; and though he could not continuously exercise his functions in Scotland (since he was also Founder and Head of the Legion in England), nevertheless his interest in Scottish affairs never waned. Under a series of able and capable Chairmen (Sir William Dick-Cunyngham having been lost by death after only one year in office) the National Executive Committee continued its work in accordance with the Constitution and gradually expanded and developed its scope. To deal adequately with this work in all its phases would fill far more pages than the writer is allowed. Moreover, to do so in any great detail would make this narrative unutterably boring to the average member of the Legion who, it is piously hoped, will read this book when it is published. Therefore the plan will be to relegate to Appendices as many lists, tables, figures, etc., as may be possible, thus leaving the story to stand out clearly.

The National Executive Committee was guided in all its decisions by the terms of the Constitution which was drawn up in the first year of its existence. Summarising the purpose of the British Legion, it might be said to be this :

To unite under one head all the men and women who served in any branch of the Services ; and to assist them, their widows and dependents in all their difficulties, in pension matters, in the relief of distress, in finding employment and in re-establishing them on their return to civilian life ; and finally to raise funds to carry on this work.

From that it will be seen that the British Legion is not, and never has been, a Benevolent Organization in the generally accepted meaning of the term, but that, notwithstanding, it is pledged to undertake a very wide range of benevolent work. (A special chapter is devoted to the connected subjects of Pensions, Employment and Resettlement, and so they will only be lightly outlined here.)

Probably the earliest and most pressing task which the Legion had to tackle was that of helping the returning men (or their widows or dependents) to obtain their due pensions. The soldier, as ever, understood nothing of

The portrait of our Founder, Field-Marshal
Earl Haig is the well-known one by Sir
James Guthrie, and is reproduced by kind
permission of Earl Haig. (From *The
Claymore*, Conference Number, 1950.)

Members of the National Executive Council of the British Legion Scotland and guests,
Edinburgh, 1941.

form-filling, and his womenfolk even less. They needed all the help they could be given—and let it be emphasised that it was always willingly available if they asked for it. This task, of course, could only be accomplished successfully with the goodwill and co-operation of the Ministry of Pensions in London ; and by 1924 the Legion had achieved such standing that it was invited to send representatives to interview the Secretaries of State for War and Air respectively on this highly important matter. This invitation implicitly acknowledged the Legion to be the proper representative Organization for ex-Servicemen — a notable step forward. The man primarily in charge of the Pensions Department at the beginning was Mr G. Connolly, who retired only in 1945. He organized and carried out the work connected with Pensions and Allowances so thoroughly that by 1939 over ten thousand cases had been represented at the Pensions Appeal Tribunals (Entitlement and Assessment) of which 70% were allowed. The kindred subject of Employment was also energetically attacked from the start. In the first place, public opinion had to be educated to recognize the need for giving preference to all classes of ex-Servicemen ; and secondly, the Government and Local Authorities had to be influenced into giving them statutory preference in all State and local schemes for Employment. Later on, the Legion created its own machinery for filling vacancies, and managed to place many a man in work.

Concurrently, the Legion kept a keen eye open to ensure that the terms of the King's National Roll were being observed.[1]

The procedure for convening an Annual Conference in different places, at which all areas and branches were, as far as possible, represented, was fixed in 1922, and the first of these was held at Glasgow in 1923.[2] At these Conferences many important and far-reaching Resolutions were passed which later resulted in successful action being taken by the Executive Committee on behalf of the Legion. Sometimes they even caused existing legislation to be amended (or more sympathetically interpreted) in favour of the ex-Serviceman or his widow. But these Annual Conferences possessed other virtues besides that of authorising the Executive Committee to take a certain line of action. They enabled the branch and area representatives to meet the men from Headquarters face to face and thus to understand better what was being done for them ; and they enabled the Executive (and particularly the Pensions Officer) to realize at first-hand the impact on the ex-Serviceman of the various changing rules governing his pension and allowances. This was of great value, since not every case submitted to a Tribunal came through Headquarters. Many were put up by Area Councils and Branches without ever touching Headquarters at all.

Glancing through *The Historical Record of the British Legion Scotland* compiled in 1937 on the instructions of the Publicity Committee to mark the Coronation Year, one is struck by the multiplicity of things which were attempted, and done, in those years between the wars. Quite apart from the routine work of Pensions, Allowances and Employment and its further development in step with changing circumstances, the subjects engaged included the following :—

> The convening of a Tuberculosis Committee to discuss the formation of a settlement for the treatment and after-care of Scottish tubercular ex-Servicemen.

[1] The King's National Roll was, briefly, a scheme by which various large firms undertook to employ a percentage of disabled ex-Servicemen.

[2] See Appendix C for the full list of Conferences and Conference Chairmen.

When members of the Monifieth British Legion decided that they needed an extension to their Hall, the question of finance proved a snag. Then the boys decided to do the job themselves, and now they're busy at it. Here are some of them doing a spot of spare-time bricklaying. (From *The Claymore*, November 1950.)

Mrs Maxwell Scott of Abbotsford, accompanied by (*left*) Mr F. Webster (Galashiels) and Mr Aly Marchbanks (Hawick Branch President) at 1958 Hawick Branch Annual Flower Show. (From *The Claymore*, November 1958.)

The foundation of Lady Haig's Poppy Factory in Edinburgh.

The foundation of a Publicity Committee and the publication of the British Legion Scotland Journal *Pro Patria* and a Handbook.

The adoption of a British Legion Tie.

The dedication of a pair of silk Standards presented to the Legion in 1931 by Dr. Darling of Edinburgh.

The launching of a protest against the statements in the published Memoirs of Mr Lloyd George slandering the memory of Earl Haig and Sir William Robertson (both being dead by that date, *i.e.*, 1935).

Co-operation with the British Legion in England.

Drawing up a questionnaire dealing with the " present condition of ex-Servicemen " (1936) with a view to showing the Government there were grounds for a Commission of Inquiry.

Affiliation to the British Empire Service League.[1]

But certainly one of the most sensible things the Legion inaugurated, as far back as 1924, was the Women's Section. This feature is dealt with in more detail in Chapter VI, but it is enough to say here that there are some 160 Branches of the Women's Section to-day, affiliated in the main to a British Legion Scotland Branch, of which 23 are in districts where there is not a similarly named branch. Those who read *The Claymore* will readily recognise how much their work is integrated with that of the branches, and would also agree that the photographs in its pages would tend towards a rather uninspiring uniformity were it not for the touch of feminine interest which the ladies supply.

Yet, this story of the growth of an important National Organization is not one without any setbacks. No scheme ever prospered entirely from the start, and the Legion was no exception to this rule. Quite apart from the fluctuating fortunes of its day-to-day endeavours, the year 1928 was a sad one in which death took away not only the Founder, Lord Haig, but also the General Secretary, Mr Baxter. To lose two such untiring and unselfish workers for the cause of the British Legion was a severe blow. Yet, the Legion did not crumble. It mourned its loss, filled the gaps in the ranks, and carried on as the Founder would have wished. Admiral of the Fleet Lord Jellicoe assumed the Presidency ; and Commander Newcombe was appointed General Secretary.

This is not the place in which to write an obituary notice of Lord Haig. It has already been done by some of the ablest pens in the land ; but it should always be remembered that he did not choose to allow himself any rest after five years of strenuous campaigning, but rather to give the remainder of his health and strength to the cause of the men who had served him. After he had been laid to rest in his family burying-ground at Dryburgh Abbey, with the last honours being paid by the local Branches of the Legion, somebody said, " The Legion has lost its Founder but has found its Patron Saint." The words may have been symbolical—but they were very near to the truth.

[1] The League was founded at a Conference of Empire delegates who assembled at Cape Town at Lord Haig's invitation in February 1921. (See picture on page 134.) It is an Organization uniting the ex-Servicemen of the whole Empire. The primary functions of the League are to act as an Empire Headquarters, and a clearing house for all matters concerning ex-Servicemen. (Its title was changed in 1958 to British Commonwealth Ex-Services League.)

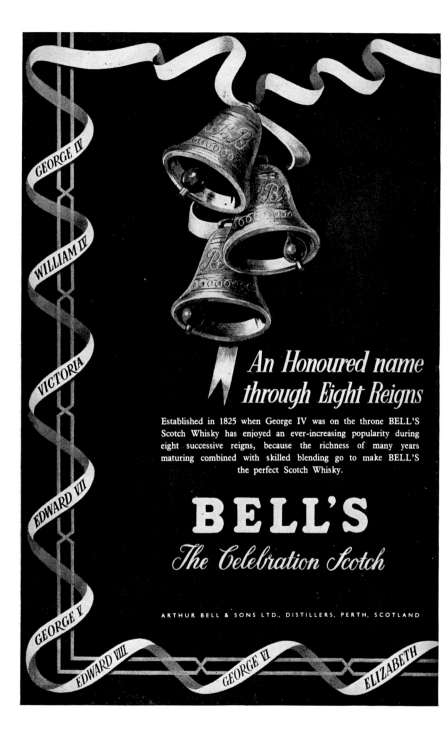

An Honoured name
through Eight Reigns

Established in 1825 when George IV was on the throne BELL'S Scotch Whisky has enjoyed an ever-increasing popularity during eight successive reigns, because the richness of many years maturing combined with skilled blending go to make BELL'S the perfect Scotch Whisky.

BELL'S
The Celebration Scotch

Only two years before his death he attended the 1926 Annual Conference at Hamilton and gave a stirring Presidential address. It was the first time he had done so, and he made a tremendous impression on the audience. His speech, recorded in longhand by the Secretary, appears in full in the original Minute Book of the Executive (1921-28). One extract from his speech (which fills ten foolscap pages in all) will be quoted here because it concerns Poppy Day, that anniversary which is such an integral part of the British Legion, and indeed of our National Year. It is quoted because it stresses two points which tend to become forgotten or overlaid in a nation-wide affair such as this :

> " *The main source of our funds is Poppy Day* ; and the success of Poppy Day is to be found in the way that all Branches of the Legion, all local Committees, and all the *Voluntary workers* come forward to help in the *most unselfish way.*"

Lord Haig's biographer says that he hated speaking in public and that he was not good at it. Nevertheless, the sincerity with which he made his long speech to the Conference that day gave wings to his words, and no practised orator could have produced a greater effect. It is true that the cause to which he was so devoted involved him in a spate of letter-writing and speech-making which he disliked intensely. Even so, it has been written of him that he never worked himself harder than in the last years of his life. "Service, Not Self!" was not only his slogan, but his way of life.[1]

His successor, Admiral Lord Jellicoe, was only able to fill the post for a few years before he resigned in 1931, whereupon the National Executive Council invited General Sir Ian Hamilton to become President, an invitation which, to the delight of all members, he accepted. No better choice could have been made. He was a gallant, distinguished and well-known soldier, a gifted writer and speaker whose charm of manner endeared him to all.

The Annual Conference at Inverness in 1931 brought before the delegates two of the most popular personalities of the day—the Prince of Wales and Sir Ian—and the future of the Legion seemed bright with the promise of strong and popular leadership.

There was still one ever-recurring problem that had never been resolved. It was a matter of policy in which even the great Field-Marshal himself had failed to achieve the unity he so much desired to see. This was the problem of amalgamation with the (younger but larger) British Legion in England, a project which had been often explored but which generally became wrecked on financial rocks. Now, however, the question was formally raised (as it happened, for the last time), and a referendum was made to all branches on the subject. The result was a clear vote against amalgamation, and so the idea was dropped. Nevertheless, a Special Committee was appointed in 1928 to form a basis for closer co-operation with the Legion in England, and this liaison has been mutually profitable ever since. One result has certainly been that those in Scotland are able to participate in overseas War Graves Pilgrimages organized by the Legion in England, an opportunity which is very much valued.

All the outside activities of the Legion during these years were aimed at educating the public to realize that the Legion was a sober, democratic, and intensely patriotic body of citizens, willingly working for the good of their comrades who had served with them in war or in peace. But although the

---

[1] A Memorial Plaque, subscribed for by all branches, was later installed in the National War Memorial at Edinburgh Castle.

. . . an atmosphere
of quiet dignity
and charm
excellent cuisine
deligthful service.

The Restaurant

HENDERSONS
OF SAUCHIEHALL STREET

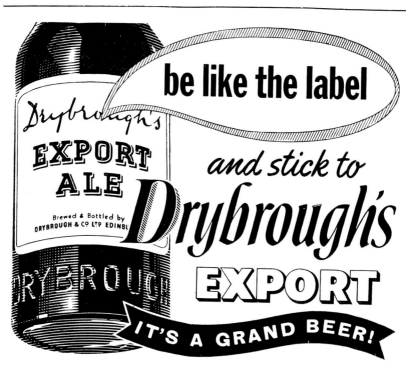
18

young serving soldier was eligible for membership, he seldom joined his local branch, because he naturally felt somewhat small in the company of his elders who could talk (and *did* talk) of the hardships and dangers of a campaign which was being fought while he was at school. Not all the smart appearance of the old be-medalled soldiers on Armistice Day parades, and the Legion Standard-bearers at the Edinburgh Castle Annual Commemorative Service for the Fallen, persuaded him that the Legion would also shoulder his own troubles in due course. It was a pity, for otherwise the Legion's numbers would have been appreciably increased between the wars. Somehow the branches seem to have missed their chances and " fluffed " their propaganda.

Nevertheless, if they failed in that respect, they succeeded splendidly in their endeavours to multiply as the following comparative figures will show. In 1924 there were 231 Branches in Scotland ; and in 1936 some 300 are listed in the *Handbook*, with 8 affiliated Regimental Associations and 97 Branches of the Women's Section. This increase in strength was, of course, entirely due to personal effort, often undertaken at considerable expense to the individuals concerned. This was indeed the perpetuation of that spirit of comradeship which had animated them during the war. Colonel Norman MacLeod, one of the original Vice-Presidents of the Legion, has written about this characteristic :

> *The ex-Servicemen willing to join the Legion had to set about forming branches. One of the objects of the Legion was to maintain the comradeship which existed in the trenches. It is difficult for anyone to-day to appreciate what that was. Men were quite willing to sacrifice themselves for their fellows. For instance, if a man was detailed for duty in the trenches the night before he was going on leave, another man would come forward and ask to be allowed to take his place, as it was thought that a man was very often knocked out just before going on leave.*

> *The enthusiasm to help other men and promote branches was quite extraordinary. Night after night they went about forming new branches or helping others. Often they must have been considerably out of pocket, as they would travel to Edinburgh and pay bus fares out of their own pocket, which must have been a struggle when a man and his family were trying to live on the dole.*

So that once again it may be observed that the guiding principle of all members was " What can I contribute to the Legion ? " rather than " What shall I get out of it ? "

The year 1937 saw the British Legion Scotland well represented at the Coronation Service in Westminster Abbey by four members of the National Executive Council and their wives ; and by a contingent of 300 in the great Review of ex-Service men and women in Hyde Park on 27th June. It was typical of the President, Sir Ian Hamilton, that he and his wife should have gone to the trouble of entertaining the contingent in their London home after the parade, a kindly gesture to Scotsmen in a strange land ! And when, in July, their Majesties paid their State Visit to Edinburgh, the first unit to salute them in the streets of the Capital was a composite detachment of the Legion drawn from all over Scotland. The Legion had come far and had grown in strength until it numbered 381 Branches. It was now ready to play its part in the National Crisis which many could see, even then, was lurking only just round the corner.

J. SMART

& COMPANY (CONTRACTORS) LTD.

BUILDING AND CIVIL ENGINEERING CONTRACTORS

Glasgow & Edinburgh

CHAPTER III

THE SECOND WORLD WAR—AND AFTER

" Then it's Tommy this, an' Tommy that, an' ' Tommy, 'ow's yer soul ? '
But it's ' Thin red line of 'eroes' when the drums begin to roll—" [1]

AND by 1938 the drums were beginning to roll throughout Europe, and many were wishing that our tiny Army could be tripled in strength. Though the country had been given a respite by the Munich Agreement (so-called), there was no doubt in the minds of all thoughtful people that war with all its attendant horrors was on the way.

With a view to staving off such a disaster, the British Legion in England had organized and offered to the Government a police force, composed of Legionnaires, to supervise in a neutral capacity the Czecho-Slovakian plebiscite. On the insistence of the Scottish Chairman (Lord Airlie) a small proportion of Scots was included in the contingent which went so far as to embark, but was neither landed nor used. Thus the last chance—a slender one—of settling things peaceably was missed.

The Legion, however, prepared itself quietly for the future by maintaining a close liaison with Headquarters Scottish Command and working on a scheme for raising the personnel necessary to meet certain military requirements in the event of war. Reservists had been called up during the crisis of 1938 ; the Territorial Army was duplicating itself in numbers and establishments ; and it was clear that the Legion would soon have a wider field than ever in which to recruit members. To this end a letter went out to all Commanding Officers assuring them of the Legion's interest in the dependents of their men. It was as well to start paving the way ! Although amalgamation with the British Legion in England had made no headway, the co-operation between the two organizations became ever closer, and by the time the war started, proposals for co-operation had been agreed by the two National Chairmen and passed by their respective Executive Councils. These gave Scotland a seat on the London Central Relief Committee, and also maintained the British Legion Scotland's right to approach the Government on matters affecting Scotland, or where there was any difference in procedure.

When Mr Anthony Eden broadcast the Government's appeal for volunteers for Home Defence, members of the Legion were amongst the first to enrol and to wear the armlet of the L.D.V. (Local Defence Volunteers) on their denims—later proudly to step back into real uniform as the Home Guard.

The Women's Section also organized themselves for their part in the war effort, and they began training in elementary first aid, for which their Grand President, Her Majesty The Queen, now H.M. The Queen Mother, had presented a cup. Fortunately they were just able to conduct their annual Tour of the Cemeteries in France and Belgium before the Second

---

[1] Reprinted from Rudyard Kipling's poem *Tommy* in *Barrack Room Ballads* by kind permission of Mrs Bambridge (the author's daughter) and Messrs Methuen.

The Lost Seasons

Many of our war blinded men were country born. From our three workshops they return on holiday to the familiar scenes of their youth, but now it is only in memory that they can see the green of young corn, the summer haze on blue hills, the reds and golds of the falling leaves, or the glitter of frost and snow in the lonely glens.

Sight cannot be restored, but much can be done to brighten the lives of blinded ex-servicemen and their dependents.

Your branches can help by organising flag days, and money-making functions of all kinds. Free prizes are supplied for Whist Drives. Speakers are available for meetings. For further particulars please write to the Appeals Organiser, Newington House, Edinburgh 9.

Legacies, Deeds of Covenant, Donations
are earnestly invited by The Treasurer,

THE FUND FOR THE SCOTTISH WAR BLINDED
P.O. Box 304, Newington House, Edinburgh 9.

World War, with its fresh crop of graves, burst upon the world. It is also pleasant to be able to record, before the war overshadows this narrative, that 1939 saw for the first time some of the neighbouring English branches represented at the Border Area's Annual Service at Dryburgh Abbey to commemorate the Founder's birthday.

On the eve of war National Headquarters had moved from 7 Drummond Place to 30 St. Andrew Square, thanks to Sir William Thomson ; and the number of branches had risen to 381, with a strength of nearly 24,000. This was as well, for from the moment the war started, the Legion began a new phase of its work. Not only Headquarters in Edinburgh, but also every area council and most branches became the centre of inquiries on every conceivable subject such as " Where do I get a gas mask ? "—" How do I draw my separation allowance ? "—" My husband has been called up as a Reservist ; will his firm continue to give him anything ? "—" My husband's regiment is in Egypt, so as there is no war out there, can I join him ? " etc., etc. " Ask the Legion " became a slogan—and they seldom asked in vain. It was reckoned that about 15,000 cases altogether were handled in the early months of the war, and that by 1940 nearly 40,000 individual dependents or relatives had consulted and had been advised by the Legion, working in co-operation with other Voluntary Organizations.

There were many such voluntary enterprises in being at that time, like the War-Blinded at Newington House and Linburn, Lord Robert's Workshops, S.S.A.F.A., etc., and with each and all of these the Legion co-operated fully and generously. No boundaries were drawn : the object was the same for all, and clearly recognized as such.

Apart from the problems engendered by the war, the old enemy " Pensions " was still being energetically engaged with a measure of success, though it was noted that there was a marked decline in the number of pension cases arising out of service prior to 3rd September 1939. The pensions concerned were chiefly those payable to the widows.

The year 1940 is called the " Active Service " year of the Legion, for many of its members (including the Chairman, Lord Airlie) were back in uniform and serving overseas, thus making the work of the branches very difficult. But this was accepted as a challenge, and did not prevent their running a canteen or a concert party as required. Although the Annual Conference arranged for June had to be cancelled because of the military situation, the National Executive Council under the Vice-Chairman, Colonel Martin Kay, dealt with the Resolutions which would have been submitted to the Conference, and managed to further its own interests and the war effort in general by gaining representation on various Government Committees, while Major Pettigrew of Glasgow was included in the British Legion Committee on Employment, sitting in London. As though to illustrate that comradeship produced by mutual suffering in war can never really die, a wonderful and unexpected gift arrived in the dark days of 1940, when Britain was staggering under the biggest reverse that her arms had endured for two hundred years. It was in the form of a motor ambulance, and the donors were the British Great War Veterans of America from New York City, the comparable organization to the Legion. It seemed to suggest that we still possessed a potential ally, although another year or more was to pass over our heads before this tenuous idea became crystallized fact.

And through it all the Legion continued its own battle, dealing with 5,000 cases concerning family allowances in 1940 alone ; forming a new

Incorporated by Royal Charter in 1746

THE BRITISH LINEN BANK

offers a complete, efficient and courteous banking
service, about which you are cordially invited
to enquire at the Head Office or at any of the
two hundred Branches throughout Scotland.

The opening of accounts is equally welcomed,
whether for personal or business purposes.

HEAD OFFICE:

38 St. Andrew Square, Edinburgh.

GOVERNOR
THE RIGHT HON. THE EARL OF AIRLIE, K.T., G.C.V.O., M.C., LL.D.

DEPUTY-GOVERNOR
HIS GRACE THE DUKE OF HAMILTON, K.T., G.C.V.O., A.F.C., LL.D.

Department at Headquarters to tackle the problem of War Service Grants ; sending out 50,000 copies of an informative booklet about the Legion so that all serving men could know that their families might call on their local branch for help or advice ; and maintaining ever closer contact with England in the common quest for further improvements in pensions and allowances.

By 1941 the number of men seeking employment showed a marked increase, mainly due to men being discharged from the Services on account of their age or because of their medical category. Though it was not easy, employment was found for many of them in the Food Control Offices, the Petrol Rationing Offices, in factories and in telephone exchanges (amongst other lines of inquiry), all of which enabled younger and fitter men to be released for service. It was in that same year that the impact of Pensions for the current war began to make itself felt, and some 3,000 cases were dealt with at Headquarters alone, not counting those which were put through area and branch committees. (The expression " dealt with " often means that sound advice on pension and allowance problems was given—not necessarily that the applicant was successful.)

The Women's Section, starting the war with 118 branches, was by now soon so well known and widely respected that it was invited to send representatives to sit on all the various war committees. Never was their work so important among the fighting men's families—yet not every serving soldier, sailor or airman was a member of the Legion. In an effort to improve matters in this respect, branches were encouraged to enrol all men in their district who had been discharged from the Services, and arrangements were made whereby every man coming out of the Army received a Legion leaflet giving the address of his nearest branch.[1] Looking even further ahead, branches were sending out Honorary Membership cards in thousands to serving men in the hope that they would become full members on their return. Whether or not this recruiting policy achieved results it is difficult to say. The only membership figures available at Headquarters are based on the Capitation Grant, i.e., on the 2s. per caput (or member) forwarded by branches. On that basis of calculation, the Legion started the war in 1939 with a strength of 23,740, which in 1942 had dropped to 18,390, but by 1946 (when the bulk of demobilization was over) had reached 75,000.

Though the end of the war was by no means in sight by 1943, yet the tide had turned in our favour, and the Legion was busying itself with declaring its post-war policy to the Government and making sure that in the scramble for employment which was certain to follow demobilization, the needs of the men who had fought the war should receive preference, especially in the Civil Service and Government Departments. This, and other ideas, were incorporated in a " Declaration of Policy " which was submitted to the Prime Minister and circulated to all Members of Parliament and of the House of Lords. It was as well to keep the Government mindful of their duties towards ex-Servicemen.

The Annual Conference that year referred to the National Executive Council a Resolution about launching an appeal for funds to the public on a day to be known as " Legion Day." This, of course, could not be agreed because it was the prerogative of the Earl Haig Fund to launch a National Appeal. However, in the following year (1944) some 40,000 leaflets giving the policy of the British Legion Scotland were printed and made available

---

[1] The Royal Navy and Royal Air Force did not at first participate.

o the Services through the Scottish Churches' canteens. The leaflets ncluded an appeal composed by the President, General Sir Ian Hamilton, which ran as follows :—

> " If outposts need now guns, now food,
> The MERCHANT NAVY will make good ;

> " If there is trouble out at sea,
> There will the ROYAL NAVY be ;

> " If there is fighting on the land,
> THE ARMY (heeds not mud nor sand)
> (will be there at hand) ;

> " If these require escort or scout,
> THE R.A.F. will be about ;

> .   .   .   .

> " Their job complete ; the way home clear ;
> THE BRITISH LEGION will be here."

The 1943 Conference also took the unprecedented step of unanimously electing to Life Membership of the British Legion a foreigner in the person of the American General Dwight D. Eisenhower " in recognition of his indomitable and inspiring leadership as Commander-in-Chief of the Armed Forces of the United Nations in North Africa." (A reproduction of the actual document is on page 102.)

The impending invasion of France in June caused the cancellation of the Annual Conference as the Government had broadcast a request to minimize rail traffic, so that once again it fell to the National Executive Council to consider the Resolutions which had been put forward for the Conference. These were mainly concerned with the possible post-war problems of employment and housing. But the Legion was already turning its attention to these matters, and was maintaining a close liaison with the After-Care (War Service) Organization, and had formed a Resettlement and Employment Committee to keep in touch with all new social legislation, especially in regard to Rent Control. In fact, this Committee circularized all Members of Parliament with a view to instituting legislation which would safeguard the rights of ex-Servicemen who might have been obliged by war service to vacate their houses. The housing problem was only just beginning to show itself, but it was later to assume grim proportions. It had not reared its head after the First World War because there had been nothing like the disturbance to lives and property as had occurred in 1940-44, or the frustrating lack of building materials that followed.

Peace had now come, but the conditions of peace-time had by no means returned, and the Conference of 1945 was again concerned with keeping Ministers in far-off Whitehall informed on the many problems confronting the men returning from the Services. Resolutions were put forward by the National Executive Council to the appropriate Ministries on questions of housing, preference for ex-Servicemen being employed in Government departments, and discharges from Local Authorities, many of which influenced later legislation. In fact, the new Royal Warrant of 1945 gave effect to a number of improvements already suggested by the British Legion Scotland.[1] That body had by now become recognized as one that could

---

[1] See Chapter VII.

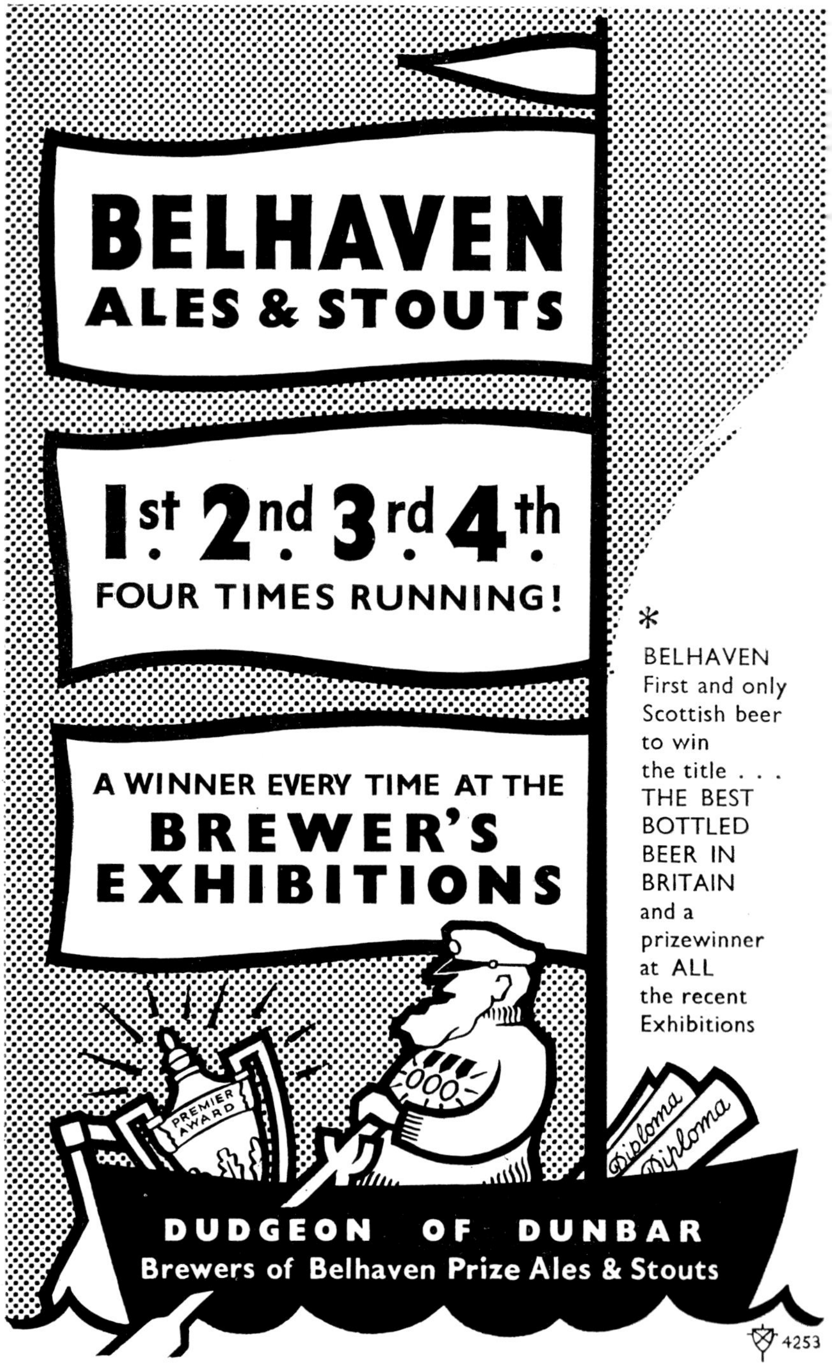

BELHAVEN
ALES & STOUTS
1st 2nd 3rd 4th
FOUR TIMES RUNNING!
A WINNER EVERY TIME AT THE
BREWER'S
EXHIBITIONS
PREMIER AWARD
Diploma
Diploma
*
BELHAVEN
First and only
Scottish beer
to win
the title . . .
THE BEST
BOTTLED
BEER IN
BRITAIN
and a
prizewinner
at ALL
the recent
Exhibitions
DUDGEON OF DUNBAR
Brewers of Belhaven Prize Ales & Stouts
4253

put forward a reasonable case for a large section of the public, and so it was only natural that the Secretary of State for Scotland should receive a Legion deputation on employment asking for preferential treatment for ex-Service fishermen. This was a difficult case to prove, and although it was listened to with attention, as yet no amending legislation has appeared.

It was decided at the Annual Conference that the original Constitution which had been drawn up in 1921, and amended in 1936, was in sore need of revision to bring it up-to-date. To help this project, " Advisers " from each Area Council were co-opted by the Sub-Committee appointed for the purpose so that the impact of the Constitution and its Rules and Bye-laws on the Areas and Branches could be better understood, and suitable amendments drawn up.

The Legion might now be said to be firmly established as a National Institution, constructed and run on sound lines, with a clearly directed policy based on loyalty to the Crown. The Press began to take notice of it, bringing its various activities to the notice of the public. An outstanding visit was when the Women's Conference in Edinburgh was opened by their Grand President.

Upon the appointment of Colonel C. S. MacLeod of Glendale as General Secretary in 1946, a complete survey of Headquarters' Staff was asked for, and recommendations were submitted to the Council for consideration. Captain R. Rowe Henry resigned, and in August 1947 Lieut.-Commander R. P. Raikes, D.S.O., was appointed Press and Publicity Officer. He resigned after two years in October 1949. Meanwhile, Captain Douglas Morton was appointed National Appeals Organizer (later changed to National Organizer) on 1st January 1949, and upon the resignation of Commander Raikes it was decided to invite Captain Morton to combine his duties as National Organizer with those of Publicity Officer. Commander Raikes was the daring Commander of the submarine *Tuna* in the war. At the personal request of the Prime Minister he had taken his ship close in to the shores of occupied France and landed parties of men in small boats to sabotage the enemy's communications. These exploits were later filmed under the title of " Cockleshell Heroes." His comprehensive scheme for publicity in Scotland included a Poster Campaign, a National Journal,[1] Christmas Cards, Diaries, advertisements in buses, etc., but before he could put all these into operation he had been offered and had accepted another appointment. The whole subject of publicity is covered in Chapter IV. The appointment of a National Appeals Organizer had been created with a view to organizing events on a national scale, and with charges for admittance which would not only attract the public and swell the funds, but would also give wide publicity to the Legion's work.

The year 1946 saw the twenty-fifth birthday of the Legion, the retirement of Lord Airlie as Chairman, of Colonel Robertson as Treasurer, and of Mr Connolly the original Pensions Officer. These gentlemen were replaced by Major-General Sir James Drew, Colonel A. A. Wighton and Mr Wood respectively. Colonel Scott, the General Secretary, also resigned about this time. Most important from a constitutional standard was the passing of a certain Resolution establishing the fact that the Conference and not the National Executive Council was the supreme authority for carrying a Resolution : thereafter the N.E.C. was bound to take action on it.

---

[1] This began as *The News Bulletin*—see Chapter IV.

Photograph by courtesy of the " Edinburgh Evening Dispatch."

Mr John Campbell, his son Jack (aged 3) and his dog " Floss " (100% War Pensioner on occupational therapy). (From *The Claymore*, Conference Number, 1950.)

Photograph by courtesy of Mr E. Sinclair, The Studio, Lerwick.

The combined Pipe Bands of the Orkney Territorial Army and Shetland British Legion leading ex-Servicemen, T.A. and R.A.F. members to Church at Lerwick for the unveiling of a Memorial Plaque to those who fell in World War II. (From *The Claymore*, October 1958.)

In that summer of 1946 Their Majesties came to Edinburgh and, amongst other engagements, reviewed 10,000 Legionnaires in the King's Park to mark the Legion's Silver Jubilee Year. It was a truly glorious occasion, and served to bring the British Legion Scotland well into the public eye. This perhaps was just as well ; for the sombre spectre of unemployment was causing great concern to all in the Legion, and public opinion was quick to see that here was a body of loyal soldier-citizens who deserved well of their country. The aim of the Legion at that time in all its Ministerial battles was to obtain preference for the ex-Serviceman in all forms of Government employment, and public opinion in their favour might well have tipped the scales in the required direction. That it did not do so must be a matter for regret. Meanwhile the solidarity of the British Legion throughout the country was confirmed by forming a joint committee with the British Legion in England, and a joint committee to administer Earl Haig's Fund.

The Annual Conference at Inverness in 1947 was, as it happened, the last one to be attended by the President, General Sir Ian Hamilton, when he was presented with the Freedom of the Burgh. In his speech of thanks he spoke of himself as being " wedded to Inverness by the traditional golden ring " (i.e., that of a Burgess). Later that year he died peacefully in London and was buried at Doune, greatly mourned by the Legion in Scotland whose members carried his personal standards and escorted his coffin to the grave. He died in the ninety-fifth year of a life which had been devoted to the service of his country, first as a serving soldier, and later as President of the Legion in Scotland. His old regiment, the Gordon Highlanders, had cause to admire him as their Colonel ; the Legion had cause to admire *and* love him as their President. To undertake a national task at the age of seventy-eight and to make a success of it for the last fifteen years of his life was an achievement of which any man might be proud. No figurehead, he was indefatigable in visiting branches, attending all important meetings of the National Executive Council, and in serving the cause of the ex-Serviceman wherever he saw his help was needed. His spirit and stamina stayed with him to the end, and it is recorded that after the ceremony of the Freedom of Inverness he lunched with the Provost, drank a large dram with the Pipe-Major and another with the Bandmaster, and then motored 150 miles back to Blair Drummond whence he had started that same morning ! The President, and at the same time the servant, of the Legion, his family motto *Addunt Robur Stirpi* " They (the branches) add strength to the root," was peculiarly apt for the task he had made his own.

He was followed in office by General Sir Thomas Riddell-Webster, who had also enjoyed a distinguished Army career which began in the Cameronians and ended as Quartermaster-General to the Forces. He is still National President at the time of publication.

The Legion now had to face two problems which were additional to those which they attacked between the wars. The first of these, publicity, has already been lightly touched on, but will be developed in Chapter IV. The other, welfare, will be examined in Chapter VII, but should be mentioned here as the early years after the Second World War were those in which it first assumed importance as a subject.

Many branches of the Legion had neither premises nor a club to which their members could resort. This curtailed branch activities considerably, as may be imagined, and tended to cause a reduction in membership. However, in 1946, a kind and generous philanthropist, Sir William Thomson, came to the Legion's rescue and offered what amounted to a blank cheque

The years between

The years between the Rebellions of the '15 and the '45 saw The Royal Bank of Scotland incorporated by Royal Charter. Since those difficult days we have served our clients faithfully in increasingly different ways—till today our service covers the most complete range of modern banking.

THE ROYAL BANK OF SCOTLAND

INCORPORATED BY ROYAL CHARTER 1727

Head Office:
ST. ANDREW SQUARE, EDINBURGH

BRANCHES THROUGHOUT SCOTLAND AND IN LONDON

ASSOCIATE BANKS:

GLYN, MILLS & CO.   **WILLIAMS DEACON'S BANK LTD.**

in interest-free loans so that branches could build or buy suitable premises or clubs. It is true that there was a certain number of ex-Servicemen's clubs scattered throughout Scotland acquired in the days before the Legion was born by grants from the Canteen Fund to the different ex-Servicemen's organizations. They were of varying repute, some being extremely respectable like the very best sort of public house, but others almost merited the advertisement displayed outside a night club which read "Good clean entertainment every night except Monday." In 1947 the British Legion Scotland took over from the United Services Fund the Trusteeship and general supervision of the surviving ex-Service clubs.

Believing that a live branch is the best form of Legion publicity, a cup won by Sir Ian Hamilton in India was presented to the British Legion Scotland for annual competition by Mrs Shield, the late Sir Ian Hamilton's secretary for many years, on behalf of Sir Ian's family. The first winners of *The Ian Hamilton Cup* were St. Andrews branch, and the present holders are Inverness branch.[1]

It might be justly said that the whole of the Legion's activities to date had been concerned with welfare; it would not be strictly true, as welfare had by now become a word with a special meaning. It covered sport and recreation by way of the branches; and it embraced rest and relaxation by means of its two Rest Homes at Shandon on the Gareloch and at North Berwick. The first was a country house called Ardgare, gifted by the owner, Colonel Sillars; and the second was a hotel bought by the Earl Haig Fund and administered by the Legion. These enterprises began in 1949 and marked a new departure in Legion activities.

During these early post-war years, four anniversaries became firm fixtures in the Legion's calendar, and served to attract public notice. The first of these was ANZAC and GALLIPOLI DAY—25th April. The Services are organized by the General Secretary on behalf of the National Executive Council at the Scottish National War Memorial in Edinburgh Castle, and are attended by representatives of the High Commissioners of Australia and New Zealand. A Legion wreath has been laid practically every year since 1950 by Mr A. J. C. Provan, himself a veteran of the Gallipoli Campaign. The second was FOUNDER'S DAY—the Sunday next before 21st June, birthday of F.M. Lord Haig. This ceremony had been inaugurated by the Border Area many years before when they paraded with their Standards at Dryburgh Abbey for a commemorative Service.

The third anniversary was in July when Scottish Command hold a Service FOR THE FALLEN at the National War Memorial in Edinburgh Castle, and three Legion Standard-bearers represent the ex-Servicemen of Scotland escorted by Guards of Honour from the three Services.

The final one of the year, of course, is REMEMBRANCE DAY.

Headquarters, now located at 23 Drumsheugh Gardens, was at this time dealing not only with Pensions, Allowances, Employment, but also with Resettlement, Emigration and Legal Advice (especially in family cases), as well as trying to help those requiring financial relief and loans for business purposes. But great difficulty was still being experienced in placing elderly ex-officers in employment. The new Legion monthly magazine *The Claymore* was started in 1950, and helped greatly in airing these activities in public because copies were always sent to the Press who gladly used any item with

---

[1] A second Cup (the Kirkennan Cup) is now presented to the most active of the smaller branches by the kindness of Major-General Sir Aymer Maxwell, a former National Chairman. The present holders are North Skye.

History of Service

This book about the British Legion in Scotland is a history of SERVICE. We of Rossleigh Ltd. also point to a proud record of service—service to motorists for nearly 70 years and of such merit that the name Rossleigh is a respected household word throughout the country.

From our head office at 32 Shandwick Place and branches throughout Scotland and in Newcastle, we offer . . .

...all that is best in motoring

By Appointment To Her Majesty the Queen, Motor Engineers

5084

human appeal in it. In fact, it was reckoned that the publicity obtained in the national and provincial Press of Scotland was in the region of 4,000 clippings (text and pictures) per annum.

The skies were darkened again in 1950 by the war in Korea and by troubles on a large scale in Malaya. So threatening did the international situation appear that the Chairman offered the services of the Legion organization to the Government if they should want them, and received a personal letter of thanks from the Prime Minister. Happily no such crisis occurred, and the Festival of Britain opened gloriously the following year. There was a Royal Review in Hyde Park to celebrate the opening, and also the thirtieth birthday of the Legion, whose members took part in the Review. As far as the Legion was concerned, this was the last time they saw their Patron, for the King died the following year, mourned not only by his own people but by half the civilized world.

The Coronation Year saw the new Queen in Edinburgh, where, amid all the attendant pageantry of that memorable week, members of the Legion played their allotted part, being represented at her arrival, at St. Giles', and in lining the route for the State Drive. The Chairman, Vice-Chairman, Hon. Treasurer together with Mr Ramsay and Brigadier Clark also represented the British Legion Scotland at the Coronation in Westminster Abbey.

Almost every year the Legion would send a delegation to see the Minister of Pensions and National Insurance, or the Minister of Labour, or the Scottish Members of Parliament, to press some point of vital interest to the Legion. They served their purpose well on the whole, and the changes in legislature and concessions granted were largely due to their persistent efforts.[1]

In 1955 the Legion lost another Chairman by the death of Major-General Sir James Drew, who had been an energetic and understanding personality at Headquarters. An able soldier in his time, he devoted all his wisdom and abilities to the Legion during his seven years in office. He was succeeded by Major-General Aymer Maxwell (later Sir Aymer).

The Legion continues to work for the good of its old comrades and their dependents. It has been founded firmly on the rock of comradeship, has never lacked able and willing leaders, and, no matter whose guiding hand is at the helm, its course and its policy will remain the same. " Service, Not Self ! " has brought it a long way in difficult seas—it will take it much further.

[1] See Chapter VII.

it's a well known

fact that

anything to do with

thread is

something to

do with

J. & P. COATS LTD · CLARK & COMPANY

CHAPTER IV

THE GUIDING MIND

"Aequam memento rebus in arduis servare mentem."
(Keep calm in troubled waters.)

HAVING outlined the history, development, and general work of the British Legion Scotland since its formation in 1921, the writer's aim is to devote the remaining chapters to describing in rather more detail some of the aspects of the Legion's organization and its activities which have already been mentioned.

The first National Headquarters was situated at 28 Rutland Street, Edinburgh, where it remained until 1924. It originally consisted of a National Executive Committee, Welfare, General Purposes and a Finance Committee ; and, in addition, a Pensions Committee, all under the National Chairman, with a full-time General Secretary and Assistant Secretary. There was also a Pensions Department under a permanent official. The offices remained in Rutland Street for only two years, after which they were moved to various Edinburgh addresses as under :

1926. 41 Albany Street.
1930. 7 Drummond Place.
1940. 30 St. Andrew Square.
1948. 23 Drumsheugh Gardens.

The present building, Haig House, has the very great advantage of accommodating under the same roof a number of Organizations with which the Legion works, notably

The Earl Haig Fund.
The Royal Artillery Association.
The Royal Air Force Association.
The Soldiers', Sailors' and Airmen's Families' Association.
The King George's Fund for Sailors.
The Officers' Association.
The Scottish Society for Employment of Ex-Regular Soldiers, Sailors and Airmen.
The Edinburgh Motor Car Park Attendants' Scheme.
(This employs only ex-Servicemen.)

Originally the Headquarters was concerned mainly with Resettlement, Pensions and Allowances, partly in handling such cases as had been referred directly to the Secretary and not dealt with by a branch, and partly in keeping a vigilant eye on all legislation bearing on the subject, and ensuring that the Legion's interests were not forgotten. All decisions were made by the National Executive Council, which Council also dealt with national and policy matters, fixed the venue for the Annual General Conference and made the arrangements for it, maintained close liaison with the Legion in England, and conducted all the general administration and also the outside affairs of the British Legion in Scotland.

Photograph by courtesy of Iain Wight, 50 Millgate Loan, Arbroath.

The Legion window during the 1958 Arbroath Civic Week. (*L. to r.*) Brigadier J. A. Oliver, Provost D. A. Gardner, Mr James Gray, Mr Tom Matheson, Mr Wm. Macdonald, Mr James Riley and Lieut.-Colonel Dunn. (From *The Claymore*, July 1958.)

The Old Soldiers show 'em all during the March Past at the 1957 Annual Conference held in St. Andrews. Not a man out of step ! (From *The Claymore*, July 1957.)

When, later on, Employment became a serious issue, Headquarters organized its own machinery for individual job-finding while still maintaining constant touch with the Ministry of Labour, firms belonging to the King's Roll scheme, and the Trades Unions.

As regards the Annual Conference, it was always the National Executive Council's duty to take appropriate action on any Resolution which the Conference passed, and this frequently meant making representations to the Ministries either by letter or by delegation. This duty the Executive Council has always conscientiously carried out. Moreover, the Council have zealously tried to be " one move ahead " of any impending legislation, so as to be able to warn areas and branches of what was being projected.

Following the Second World War, Welfare, Sport and Publicity became prominent among the Legion's activities. To give adequate attention to these new interests as well as to the old-established ones of Pensions and Employment, it was decided to appoint a Publicity Officer in 1947 and a National Appeals Organizer in 1949 (both already referred to). His first object was to make money.

Although it may be true that " money doesn't get you more friends, but it certainly gets you a better class of enemy," there can be no doubt that a sound bank balance is an essential to any philanthropic organization. His second object was the publicity for the Legion's work which the presentation of National events would obtain. The field of endeavour was a difficult one as other organizations were already extensively arranging " paid admission " events, while the areas and branches had long been accustomed to raise their local funds in this way, and the last thing Headquarters wished to do was to appear to trespass on their ground. Therefore the Organizer, treading delicately, began to arrange such affairs as exhibition Golf Matches between well-known players, Ice Rink Carnivals, Boxing Matches, Dinner/ Dances, Children's Dances, Pageants, Fêtes, Athletic Meetings, Exhibitions, etc. All of these were of direct interest to the public, who responded well— as they always have—to this fresh call from the Legion. To add extra weight, advice and help in this new venture, a National Advisory Committee was formed, under the Chairmanship of the National President, consisting of people from outside the Legion who nevertheless had its interests at heart. National Executive representatives were also included on it, so that its construction was " catholic " in the true sense of the word.

A list of Patrons of National Events was compiled which included influential persons in all walks of life, the heads of the three Services, and civic dignitaries. This engendered confidence in the general public and ensured their support. But sometimes, it is sad to record, their confidence and support proved to have been misplaced. It is said that " climate is what you *should* have, but weather is what you get ! " Well, there was the occasion when Peter Thompson and Bobby Locke played in an exhibition match at Aberdeen to only a faithful few in torrential rain ! Learning the hard way by incurring a few mishaps of this nature, the Committee wisely decided that our local weather was too unpredictable to warrant the holding of outdoor events and therefore settled for confining National projects to indoor affairs such as Balls, Mannequin Parades, Theatre performances, Film Shows and Concerts. A Working Committee was formed from the National Advisory Committee and, under the Chairmanship of Lieut.-Colonel The Hon. David Balfour, relentlessly pursued all ideas that might be profitable. Perhaps the most notable of these was the Presentation Day Ball in the Edinburgh Assembly Rooms which was held each year that the

Napier of Edinburgh

" Herbs and your Health "

The name of " **NAPIER** " in Scotland, dates back to the times when the Celtic Earls of Lennox held sway in the early 1200's. To-day, the name is associated in the Herbal World, with this firm established nearly 100 years ago, in 1860 ! !

Since it was founded, as the first Herbalist Establishment in Edinburgh, the family of Napier have continued to own and direct the business.

John R. Napier, the grandson of the founder of the business, is a fully qualified and registered Consultant Herbalist, Member of the British Herbalists' Union, and Member of the Institute of Naturapathic Physicians.

D. NAPIER & SONS devote their attention to the collecting and preserving of Medicinal Plants, their preparation into Medicines, and the knowledge of their true value in the treatment of disease.

They have a complete stock of all the British and Foreign Herbs in daily use numbering over 2,000 items which includes a great variety of the rarer and more unusual ones, comprising the widest selection of any in Scotland.

They also hold a large variety of Spices and Herbs used in Cooking, which may be had either in the whole form or powder.

Your inquiries are invited, and a Booklet describing some of their preparations may be had on request.

D. NAPIER & SONS

British and Foreign Medical Botanists
and Consulting Herbalists

15-17-18 Bristo Place, Edinburgh 1

Sovereign gave a Presentation Party in the Palace of Holyroodhouse. A strong Committee, led each year by a different lady well-known in the social world, produced a Ball which ranked in splendour with anything that the beautiful Assembly Rooms had ever seen. It is sad that Court Presentations have now ended, thus removing the *raison d'être* for this Ball.

Another attractive annual event is the Mannequin Parade sponsored yearly by Messrs Greensmith Downes of Princes Street, Edinburgh. These are staged in Edinburgh and St. Andrews, and they certainly draw an interested female audience full of enthusiasm to see a preview of the season's fashions.

Still pursuing all possible indoor attractions, a successful theatrical enterprise called " The Masque of Scotland " was presented for a week in Glasgow in St. Andrew's Hall. Written by Dr. Stewart Black and produced by John Martin, it was such a dramatic and spectacular history of Scotland that it also played for a week in connection with the Festival of Britain. Glasgow Area, like other areas and branches when events were held in their districts, helped generously with this.

Not quite on the same lines, but again a novelty for the public, were the Exhibition of the Royal Tour in 1955, and the Exhibition of Scottish Heraldry in 1950. Both were full of interest and beautifully arranged, the first in the Signet Library and the second in the Merchants' Hall, and both were well noticed by the Press.

The Working Committee examined all possible variations of a scheme such as the Irish Hospitals Sweepstake, and eventually hit on the idea of organizing a " Competition of Skill " in connection with the Derby which would not only come within the law but would raise the funds considerably. In 1956 the prize was a new Car presented by the Standard Motor Company ; and a valuable publicity note was struck by Marshal of the Royal Air Force Lord Tedder, Chairman of that Company, presenting the car to Miss Vivien Leigh, who was photographed accepting it on behalf of the Legion. One would have thought it was difficult, if not impossible, to name the first four horses in the Derby, but oddly enough this miraculous feat has been accomplished by somebody each year. The organization necessary at Headquarters to sort some 40,000 coupons is considerable, and a special " Volunteer Force " has to be enlisted for this purpose each year ; but there can be no doubt that this event spreads publicity for the Legion's work far and wide throughout Scotland.

Yet, even with all these methods of raising money, the funds were never altogether adequate for the Legion's purposes, largely due to the constant rise in the price of everything. Debarred from making a direct appeal to the public on behalf of the Legion by reason of Earl Haig's Fund prerogative in this field, the National President, General Riddell-Webster, in 1956 started an Appeal to branches to allocate a certain percentage of the profits of any event to National Headquarters.

Of course the " power of the Press " is widely recognized, and it is the business of the Publicity Officer to exploit this vis-a-vis the National and Provincial papers and also towards members of the Legion. To-day *The Claymore*, issued monthly, is the instrument of this policy—but it did not begin publication until 1950. Before that there had been various publications of a different nature giving news of the Legion's activities both to its members and to the outside world. As far back as 1924 it was decided that Scottish notes should be forwarded to London each month for inclusion in *The British Legion Journal*, but this was evidently an unsatisfactory

arrangement, and in 1925 the Secretary was instructed to consult printers about a Scottish Journal. The result was a publication called *The British Legion Scotland Journal*, later changed to *Pro Patria* with a picture of Lord Haig on the cover. Under one or other of these titles, this magazine appeared until the outbreak of war in 1939. After the war, it was only possible to publish a *News Bulletin* owing to the cost of paper, and this continued until 1950, when the Publicity Officer was authorised to produce and publish *The Claymore*, whose contents would have a wider interest for its readers. *The Claymore*, with its illustrated notes on branch activities, its reports of the Executive Council Meetings, of the Annual Conference, of the latest news on Pensions and Allowances, Employment, Resettlement and Sport, and Branch and Area events, in addition to general articles and the ever-useful " Letters to the Editor," has now become the official channel of communication between National Headquarters and its areas and branches.

It goes to all the Press in Scotland and they generously give support by quotations from its paragraphs. It also goes to all Scotsmen serving in the Armed Forces through their Canteens, their Chaplains, and the British Red Cross, so that it reaches them whether they are at duty or in hospital. Close liaison was early established, and has been continually maintained, with Scottish Command Headquarters, not only as to potential members, but with particular regard to a Legion stall which they kindly allot at all Army displays.

Little has been said so far about Sport, but it holds a prominent place among the activities of all areas and branches. National Headquarters organizes six Competitions for eight trophies which are competed for by the nine areas. The following list shows the details :—

> *The Rintoul Trophy*—for Billiards.
> Given by J. B. Rintoul, Esq.
>
> *The Houldsworth Trophy*—for Snooker.
> The gift of Colonel Sir Thomas Houldsworth, Bart., President, Ayrshire Area.
>
> *The " Daily Record " Trophy*—for Darts (fours).
> Presented by *The Daily Record*.
>
> *The Murray Trophy*—for Darts (singles).
> Donated by William Murray & Co.
>
> *The Samuel Coronation Trophy*—for Darts (pairs).
> Presented by H. Samuel Ltd.
>
> *The Erskine Hill Trophy*—for Bowls.
> Given by J. Erskine Hill, Esq.
>
> *The Dunedin Trophy*—for Golf.
> Donated by Edinburgh Area Council.
>
> *The Wighton Trophy*—for Curling.
> Presented by Colonel A. A. Wighton, formerly Honorary National Treasurer.

In addition to these, there are four other trophies which are presented by Headquarters. The first two used to be won by the branch and area scoring the highest aggregate of points at the National Athletic Meeting, but

44

since the abandonment of that event, they are now awarded on the following conditions :—

The National Playing Fields Cup.—Won annually by the branch adjudged to have done most to foster Sport. Presented by the National Playing Fields Association.

The Stuart Trophy.—Won annually by the area adjudged to have done most to foster Sport among its branches. Given by Mr A. S. Stuart, Chairman, Edinburgh and Lothians Area.

Apart from Sport, there is *The Eglinton Trophy*, presented to the branch whose Colour-bearer wins the Annual Colour-carrying Competition at the Annual Conference. The gift of J. Walker, Esq.

Believing as it does that a flourishing branch is the best advertisement for the Legion, National Headquarters does everything in its power to encourage the growth and well-being of branches throughout Scotland without interfering with their activities in any way. At the same time it handles the National affairs of the Legion, the interests of all ex-Servicemen, and ensures publicity for its great and abiding work.

The accompanying diagram, as minuted by the National Executive in 1951, shows (with names added) how Headquarters is organised to do this work.

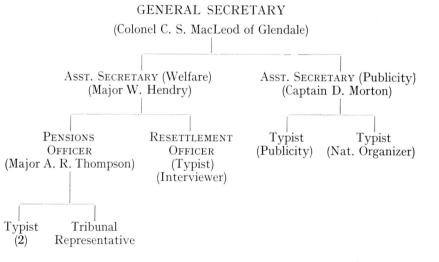

GENERAL SECRETARY
(Colonel C. S. MacLeod of Glendale)

ASST. SECRETARY (Welfare)
(Major W. Hendry)

ASST. SECRETARY (Publicity)
(Captain D. Morton)

PENSIONS OFFICER
(Major A. R. Thompson)

RESETTLEMENT OFFICER
(Typist)
(Interviewer)

Typist
(Publicity)

Typist
(Nat. Organizer)

Typist
(2)

Tribunal
Representative

A War-time March Past for the Conference in the days of gas-masks.

A " pocket-sized " Queen! Silvia D. Dow, Crieff, in the Branch's Fancy Dress Parade in 1953. (From *The Claymore*, October 1953.)

Members of the British Legion Czecho-slovakian Police Force on board their transport in the River Thames, 1938. (From *The Claymore*, January 1953.)

CHAPTER V

THE LUSTY LIMBS

" They go from strength to strength."

FROM Lerwick in the Shetlands to Gatehouse-of-Fleet, from Lossiemouth to Lochalsh, the branches of the British Legion cover Scotland and take their place in the community life of their districts. In just under forty years the British Legion in Scotland has risen from a dozen or so branches to some 420, with some 160 Women's Sections—a reflection of the comradeship unity of purpose engendered by two World Wars.[1]

This rather startling result was not achieved without a considerable amount of hard work, often on the part of some public-spirited individual who had seen the need for a branch and had taken the time and the trouble to start one. Colonel Norman MacLeod has been quoted elsewhere for the statement that these keen individual members would, in the early days, come into Edinburgh and Glasgow at their own expense in order to find out how to constitute a branch, and would then return to their district and spend many an evening visiting old comrades and personally persuading them to found a branch. They felt it essential to revive and maintain that comradeship that had been born in the trenches and at sea ; and they felt too, that in a shaky world, men with that sense of living in and for a community and its ideals might play a useful part in their local affairs. And it was not long before they were proved right.

But first, the ambitious Legionnaires would have to obtain the approval of their local area committee before forming their branch. At the earliest meeting of the British Legion in Scotland it was decided that the branch should be the unit, but it was also accepted that a measure of decentralization was necessary in the general administration of such branches. It was hoped and intended to cover all Scotland, and therefore the country was divided into geographical areas, each under a council responsible to the National Executive for the conduct and general administration of its own branches. The number of areas has varied from time to time. Seven were formed in the very early days, and this number was soon increased to nine. Later (somewhere in the nineteen-thirties) it rose to eleven, but eventually returned to nine, a figure which seemed to cover Scotland satisfactorily. The principle has always been that the area council was elected at the Annual General Meeting of the branch delegates of the area, so that all branches should have a voice in the election of their council and in the conduct of Legion affairs within the area. In these councils the Secretary was the main channel of communication between branches and National Headquarters. To him fell the task of building up the area by encouraging the growth of new branches, the duty of organizing the various sports competitions, as well as the general secretarial work. He has always dealt with claims for Disability Pensions, and has ever been ready to collect evidence and offer advice on how to appeal against a harsh assessment. Depending upon the situation

---

[1] See Appendix E for list of areas and branches.

SHEETS
PILLOW CASES
AND TOWELS

express to perfection
the lasting quality of
Scottish-made textiles

The range includes the splendid

TARTAN TOWELS
in the authentic Clan Tartans

JAMES FINLAY & COMPANY, LIMITED
22 WEST NILE STREET - - GLASGOW, C.1.

of his office and his own standing in his community, the area secretary has frequently found himself appearing on behalf of members to give evidence before Panels and Courts of Reference, and has even been appointed a member of a local Tribunal. Since the last war, he has learned so much about Employment, Housing and Resettlement that he may well be in constant touch with the County Clerk, and even be a member of the local Employment Committee, depending upon conditions in his area. Conditions, of course, vary very greatly as between areas. Before motoring and motor buses became general, visiting outlying branches used to take up much of a secretary's time. In a rural area he would seldom be able to visit one and return to his home the same night. In fact one secretary recorded that in 1949 he spent 76 nights of the year away from his home on this particular duty. Another travelled 166 miles in one month alone on ordinary Legion business such as Pensions, Resettlement, Meetings, etc., in addition to writing more than 300 letters from his office. Yet another area secretary "logged" a hundred visits or interviews extending over three months as a typical quarter's work, and the following notes taken at random from his log-book give an idea of the diversity of his cases.

Engineer, sacked, redundant, wants job but won't leave district—difficult.

Saw three doctors re a man's pension claim.

Ex-Service lady, domestic trouble, recommended to a solicitor.

Entry secured for boy to go to Royal Caledonian School, Bushey.

Eight Prince of Wales Pensions applicants in one day.

Pension obtained for applicant—letter of thanks.

Witnessing certificates.

Ex-Serviceman keen to settle down South—contacts.

Hospital forms obtained.

Mother brings in letter from Ministry of Pensions re her son—very disturbed.

Claim for medals and gratuity attended to.

Can son get into R.A.F. ?—4' 10" and not likely to grow much.

Domesticity again—son, foot crushed at work. Father killed in Royal Navy. Mother re-married.

Ex-Serviceman ordered to give up house—solicitor did not turn up when case called—seven days to quit. What then ? S.S.A.F.A. request particulars of case.

Son refused to go into hospital for diagnosis—terrible—no one to blame but mother.

Served Royal Naval Boom Defence, 1943—pension turned down—difficult bloke of instructor type—he knows it all.

Ex-Serviceman complains about school appointment. Inter-denominational matter ?

And so on, multiplied by four to complete a year's work, or by thirty-six for the nine areas of Scotland. The area secretary has become by experience a man of wide qualifications, and a guide, philosopher and friend to all in his area, whether or not they are members of the Legion.

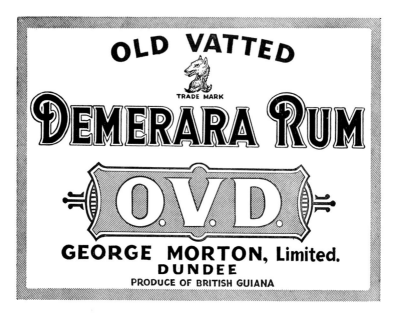

Branches, of course, were virtually in existence before areas were designated as such, though they were for the most part clubs and associations of Old Comrades under one name or another. Where club premises existed it was comparatively easy to form an association around such a club which later became a branch of the British Legion. Which was the first of these branches? According to the records of the Ayrshire Area Council, which go back to its first meeting in 1921, there are six branches in that county which can claim this honour. At that meeting of 1921 there were two delegates from each of the six branches of the Comrades of the Great War which had formed in the county in 1920.[1] The meeting considered a circular letter from the National Council in Edinburgh convened by Field-Marshal Lord Haig which proposed that all existing ex-Service organizations should amalgamate within the British Legion Scotland, and the delegates from the six Ayrshire branches agreed to this proposal. It is equally possible, though unrecorded at the time of publication, that other branches in Scotland took the same action in the same year; but the fact is that the earliest date for *any* branch (including the six Ayrshire ones) as recorded at National Headquarters, is 1926. Yet in Edinburgh, also, as will be seen from the photograph on page 132, similar early meetings took place. Mr Alex. Stuart, chairman of the Edinburgh and Lothians Area for a good many years and still in office, was one of the movers of that meeting, so the Capital city also was well in the lead from the very start. Nevertheless, in 1921, it was reported at the first Unity Conference that there were over 100 branches of ex-Service organizations throughout Scotland affiliated to the Legion. The assumption is that no proper form of registration was in existence until 1926.

Be that as it may, the branches flourished wherever they were planted, and obviously fulfilled the need for ex-Servicemen to congregate, firstly in order to exchange campaign stories and have a social evening, secondly to help their less fortunate comrades as need arose, and thirdly to remember publicly each Armistice Day those who had died. At least one branch established an overseas liaison, as a letter from the Memorable Order of Tin Hats in Durban in 1935 to the Montrose Branch renewing greetings shows. Gradually these branches developed other activities between the two wars, and where there was an active club this tended to become a social centre for all the men of the community. Sports, outings, Burns suppers and social evenings to which ladies were admitted, gave the Legion a special place in community life and probably encouraged the women to form a branch also. Where such was the case, the parent branch was undoubtedly enabled to widen its field of activities. For those branches which had no premises the first step was to obtain some, and here they were assisted by a loan from National Headquarters which was made available, free of interest, by that generous philanthropist, Sir William Thomson.[2] Many branches were so strong that they owned a pair of Colours and a Pipe Band, and so well organized that they formed sub-committees to handle their sporting activities, and even to deal with certain of their own pensions affairs. These were in a sound position when the Second World War came, for many of their members were by then too old for active service, and thus remained available to carry on the good work of their branch. Not all branches were so fortunate however, especially where circumstances had caused a decline in the population and potential membership after the war; so that although

[1] Dalry, Galston, Girvan, Kilmarnock, Maybole and Tarbolton.
[2] Altogether Sir William lent £10,500 for this purpose. After his death the scheme was carried on by National Headquarters itself.

By Appointment
To Her Majesty The Queen
Biscuit Manufacturers
McVitie & Price, Ltd.

Say . . .

"McVitie's"

the word before

Biscuits

★

Made by
McVITIE & PRICE LIMITED
Edinburgh   London   Manchester

the membership of the Legion as a whole was vastly increased by a new generation, the centre of gravity in various communities had shifted so much that many a branch could barely exist. Some in fact became dormant, and even died; but wherever the returning warriors felt the need of a branch, you might be sure that one would arise. Probably guided by the " old hands " on sound lines, it was not long before the new generation began to assume the responsibility for the management of branch affairs, as the result of which the activities showed an increase in scope and diversity. Times had changed; darts began to oust billiards; golf (at any rate in the East) became a branch and area competition; dances were popular as well in the community as in the club; a fancy dress carnival and a beauty queen contest became regular events of the summer, and the local Legion branch, moving with the times, became an essential part of civic life. And as Remembrance Day and Founder's Day came round each year, the main source of colour came from the Legion Standards and the Legion Pipe Bands. Soon the Legion, by its example, became recognized as a power for good throughout Scotland. " A good branch is the best advertisement for the Legion." This maxim was accepted long ago, and was recognized by the presentation in 1946 of a cup [1] for the most progressive branch won by annual competition. The judging of this contest is a really difficult task, as the answers to numerous different headings given on a printed form have to be considered. Membership, meetings, social and sporting and charitable activities, Poppy Day collection, subscriptions to *The Claymore*—all these and many more topics come under consideration before the award is made. And since it is realized that local situations are so varied and exercise such a vast influence on the prosperity of branches, a second cup [2] for the best of the small branches has been given by Major-General Sir Aymer Maxwell, a former National Chairman. All of which tends to ensure that branches do not remain content to rest on their laurels, but strive to improve in numbers and quality.

There is certainly not one month in the year—and probably not one week either—in which a well-run branch is idle. The illustrated pages of *The Claymore* feature their activities every month and show what a wide field they cover. Allowing for additions or alterations according to locality, a typical branch calendar might read thus :

January.   Burns Night Supper.
           Area Curling Competition.
           Dances.
           Branch Annual General Meeting.

February.   Curling.
           Area Annual General Meeting.
           Darts.
           Billiards.
           Whist Drives.
           Dances.

March.   Darts.
           Billiards.
           Whist Drives.
           Dances.

[1] The " Ian Hamilton " Cup.   See Chapter IV.
[2] The " Kirkennan " Cup.

Photograph by courtesy of A. G. Ingram Ltd., Edinburgh.

The 1951 Remembrance Day Service, Usher Hall, Edinburgh. In front, the boys from Queen Victoria School, Dunblane. (From *The Claymore*, January 1952.)

Photograph by courtesy of the " Perthshire Advertiser."

" Old Bill" Rides Again ! A picture full of reminiscence for the 1914-18 old soldier. Members of the Crieff Branch during their Legion Week. (From *The Claymore*, October 1952.)

54

April.	Golf.
	Bowls.
	Area Council Meeting.
May.	Area Golf Competition.
	Bowls.
	Train Standard-Bearers for Annual Competition.
	Organize Stand at Agricultural Show.
June.	Annual Conference.
	National Colour-Bearing Competition.
	Beauty Queen Contest.
	Founder's Day Service.
July.	Annual Outing.
	Area Bowls Competition.
	Fancy Dress Carnival.
August.	Outing for War Disabled Hospital Patients.
September.	Pipe Band Engagements at Local Games.
October.	Darts Competitions.
	Billiards.
	Carpet Bowls.
	Children's Hallowe'en Party.
November.	Poppy Week Collection.
	Remembrance Day Service and Parade.
	Darts, Billiards, Whist and Dancing.
December.	Inter-Branch Night.
	Children's Christmas Party.

That rough outline takes no account of the various social activities in the winter months, many of them in conjunction with the Women's Section, such as lectures, film shows, etc., which are often a regular weekly feature of the winter programme. And thus the branches have prospered and multiplied to the benefit of their members and their neighbourhood, and, let it be said, to the good of Scotland. Their members have added yet another distinction to the profession of arms so that it may be truly said of each one : " This is the happy warrior, this is he that every man in arms should wish to be."

"You can't get along without me"

SAYS DAISEE JUTE

"You can't get along without jute" claims Daisee. Not being vain. Jute's modest, if ever anything was. It's at work everywhere, unhonoured, unsung. Doing jobs so important you take them for granted.

The humble, necessary sack, for instance, is jute. So is the core of wire rope and electric cables. And a lot of twine and cord and twist and string. You walk in jute and under jute and on jute. It's the lining of your suit; it's roofing felt; it's the basis of carpets, and the backing of linoleum.

Ubiquitous, that's jute. You might be able to *exist* without it, just. But you certainly couldn't *live* in any sort of comfort.

Can jute help you? If you think jute in any form can solve your problem, write to us. We'll be glad to advise.

JUTE INDUSTRIES LTD.

Britain's Largest Makers of Jute Goods

MEADOW PLACE BUILDINGS · DUNDEE

CHAPTER VI

OUR BETTER HALVES

*" No matter how hard a man may labour, some woman is always
in the background of his mind—she is the one reward of Virtue."*

IT is not generally realized that the Women's Section of the British Legion
came into being in 1921, although its official recognition was not granted
until 1924. It was formed with the dual purpose of safeguarding the
interests of the widows, dependents and families of men who had served in
the Forces, and also of augmenting and widening the activities of the British
Legion. To-day, after thirty-five years of active work, the Women's Section
can proudly claim to have achieved both its objects. Its Grand President
is H.M. The Queen Mother.

There are few satisfactory results that are not obtained without some
preliminary setbacks, and the development of the Women's Section was no
exception to this well-known rule. Though its members had been devotedly
carrying on their welfare work during the First World War and after it,
they had done so through the various organizations which were then in
existence, such as the Comrades of the Great War, the National Federation
and the National Association of Discharged and Demobilized Sailors and
Soldiers. When, therefore, these organizations became merged in the
British Legion in 1921, the Women's Section naturally assumed the same
title. They continued to work as they had before, but as an autonomous
body under their own rules and without reference to the Constitution of
the British Legion. This apparent anomaly caused some misunderstanding
and confusion, and in order to regularize matters the National Executive
Council appointed a sub-committee consisting of Colonel Norman Macleod
and Doctor Shiels to meet Mrs Thomson and Mrs Weir for discussion. The
Legion representatives referred to the Constitution and gave their opinion
that in accordance with Rule 4, " any women's organization using the name
' British Legion ' in its title or carrying on its work, directly or indirectly,
under the auspices of the British Legion, was not, and never could be, a
separate and independent organization, but must in general conform to the
Constitution."

The ladies generously accepted this principle, and the result was that
the Constitution and Bye-Laws for the Women's Section of the British
Legion in England [1] were carefully examined and finally adopted for the
Women's Section in Scotland also. Official recognition followed immediately,
and warm appreciation of their work was expressed. There can be no doubt
that the step taken that day was a realistic and popular one which has
certainly " augmented and widened the work of the British Legion."

Until her death in 1939, Lady Haig as Patroness took a keen interest in the
affairs and activities of the Women's Section. In 1926 Lady Haddington,
who is still in office, was appointed President, and has always given practical
support for the various projects recorded in this chapter. Mrs Thomson,

---

[1] The British Legion Scotland, about eight years ago, revised the Bye-Laws of
its own Women's Section.

R. & W. Sorley Ltd.

R. & W. SORLEY LTD.

Jewellers and Silversmiths

107-9 West George Street

Glasgow, C.2

Cen 8951

Established 1819

Chronometer and Watch Makers
to the Admiralty

BILSLAND'S bake BETTER BREAD

who had negotiated with the British Legion on the constitutional question became the first Chairman, and it was largely due to her energy and enthusiasm that the Women's Section achieved such splendid results in submitting cases of hardship among ex-Service men and women after the First World War. It was, of course, that " family " aspect of their work on which they were primarily engaged, and in doing so they brought great influence to bear on public opinion which was gradually won over to the support of the Legion and its work. Without public opinion behind it, the British Legion could accomplish little—and it is due in no small measure to the Women's Section that this source of support is solidly there.

But not all their work lay in the " family " field. At their Annual General Conference in 1949, Lady Haddington proposed the idea of donating a house at Linburn for the use of the Scottish National Institution for the War Blinded. With the warm approval of all the delegates present she launched an appeal for funds. The branches, true to their reputation, set about the task of raising the money in their own areas by their own methods, and at the 1952 Conference Lady Haddington was able to hand over a cheque for £1,800 (later increased to £2,400) to the Chairman of the War Blinded Institution. The house was completed, handed over and occupied in May 1954. This was a really outstanding achievement, and deserves to be taken out of its historical context as it has been ; but now it is time to restore the lost chronology.

After the First World War the chief concern of all branches of the Legion—men and women—was with the inter-related problems of Pensions and Allowances, and Employment ; and there is no doubt that the Women's Section proved their worth in this unending struggle against the adversity that afflicted many families of returned soldiers. The real hard luck case would be ferreted out by a member visiting, and talking to a family, and the bare facts established often while the ex-soldier was away at work. A further visit, when the man was at home, would perhaps reveal documentary evidence of a genuine case. Thereafter it would be represented to Headquarters who would carry it on. In this sort of problem a Women's Section in a locality where there was no established branch of the Legion could—and did—bring to light many a deserving case which might otherwise never have been noticed.

It is generally true to say that women, rather more than men, are anxious to be of service to others. It must have been this characteristic that caused the Women's Section to spring up and flourish, for wherever they were formed there were always countless forms of service to be done. Their range was quite extraordinary, and it must be counted as a really fortunate break that when the Second World War came there were so many public-spirited and well organized women ready and willing to offer their part-time services wherever they were needed. Part-time it had to be, for many a woman had a home and family to care for as her primary task. Yet it was those who had been called upon to make the sacrifice of sending their men to the wars who were the keenest to be of service themselves. Here it was that the Women's Section proved so valuable as an organized body capable of absorbing all volunteers and directing their energies into the proper channels. They served in many capacities according to the needs of the moment and their own powers. Some supervised canteens, others assisted in them ; some served in the Red Cross, others in Civil Defence ; they worked on Prisoner-of-War Committees, on Comfort Funds, in soup kitchens and telephone exchanges. Wherever the need arose and a Women's Section

THE EARL HAIG FUND
(SCOTLAND)
President: Col. The DUKE of BUCCLEUCH, K.T., P.C., G.C.V.O., T.D., D.L., LL.D.

Founded in 1921 by Field Marshal Earl Haig to cover the War of 1914-18, for relief of distress among ex-Servicemen and their dependents in Scotland.

Extended in 1940, the Fund now embraces not only those who fought in the 1939-45 War but many other classes of ex-Service men and women according to circumstances.

Organized in two areas with Headquarters in Edinburgh and Glasgow respectively.

Income derived mainly from the annual Poppy Day Appeal and from donations and legacies.

Average expenditure on relief every year over £50,000.

Maintains Homes for ex-Service veterans in Edinburgh and Glasgow.

Gives a grant annually to the British Legion Scotland and Lady Haig's Poppy Factory.

Subscriptions, donations and legacies will be gratefully received, and should be sent to

THE GENERAL SECRETARY,
23 DRUMSHEUGH GARDENS,
EDINBURGH 3.

who will allocate them to the Area concerned.

THE OFFICERS' ASSOCIATION
(SCOTTISH BRANCH)
Chairman: Col. The DUKE of BUCCLEUCH, K.T., P.C., G.C.V.O., T.D., D.L., LL.D.

Part of the Officers' Association of the United Kingdom incorporated by Royal Charter.

RELIEF
Exists to relieve distress among ex-Officers and their dependants (including Women's Services and the Nursing Services) in Scotland.

EMPLOYMENT
Ex-Officers seeking employment in Scotland are advised to contact

THE EMPLOYMENT OFFICER,
1 FITZROY PLACE, SAUCHIEHALL STREET,
GLASGOW

Applications for help of a General nature should be addressed to

THE GENERAL SECRETARY,
23 DRUMSHEUGH GARDENS,
EDINBURGH 3

Space kindly gifted by

THE CULTER MILLS PAPER CO. LTD., PETERCULTER, ABERDEENSHIRE.

eard of it, that need was willingly met. Was there a sudden influx of troops to a dreary camp near their town? The local Women's Section was first in the field of organized entertainments long before E.N.S.A. could be there, running dances, whist drives and concerts for the men. Did ship-wrecked sailors, saved from their torpedoed craft, find themselves stranded in a strange town? The nearest Women's Section would at once take the first steps in providing comfort for them until the proper authorities could take over. All this—and more—they did as opportunity offered. There was almost nothing they could *not* do, including giving advice (to men who asked for it) on private affairs! It says much for their confidence in the ability of the Women's Section that they were bold enough to put forward such a request.

The war over, the ladies cast around them for more good work to do. Of course, if there was a Women's Section linked with a Legion branch, the work was not far to seek. Every branch wants to appear sociable on suitable occasions throughout the year so that it cannot be classified as simply another club "for men only," yet how many men understand the details which can make or mar a social event? Probably very few—and that was where the allied Women's Section could, and did, step in with knowledgeable hands and minds. The whist drives, dances, children's outings, sales and other events all required the expert feminine touch to make them attractive, and thus keep the Legion's name in the public mind and gain its support. Nor did the ladies confine their activities to helping only the ex-Servicemen and their families, for at different times the Women's Section has, from time to time, raised by their own efforts funds for handsome donations to the Paraplegic Coach and Comforts Funds, Lady Haig's Poppy Factory, the Thistle Foundation, the ex-Service Welfare Association for the Sick in Mind, and the British Cancer Campaign. One Women's Section, for example, raised sufficient money to endow its local hospital with an X-ray unit; and many arrange annual treats and outings for patients in Erskine Hospital, Bangour and Edenhall.

Perhaps not the least of their activities, dating from the years that followed the First World War, has been the shepherding of parties of widows and children to visit the graves of their men in France and Flanders, and now in Holland and Germany also. These visits are organized in their wider aspects by the British Legion in England and national headquarters in Scotland publicises them through *The Claymore*. The Women's Section members are always ready to help locally with the arrangements. Often bereaved themselves, these ladies can bring to this task unrivalled sympathy and understanding. They have found the truth of Adam Lindsay Gordon's lines:

> " Life is mostly froth and bubble;
> Two things stand alone—
> Kindness in another's trouble,
> Courage in your own."

The Welfare State in which we live lays great emphasis on how youth can be helped, but seems to disregard old people who are now supposed to go into a home or institution of some kind when they reach the inactive stage of life. It is true that this may sometimes be the only possible solution for them if they have no means of obtaining any help, but it is the last thing they ever wish to do. They value the personal and loving care which they know cannot be their lot in a State Institution, and the

Photograph by courtesy of Alex. Morrison, Photographer, Lumphanan.

The 1957 Winners and Cups of the Ballater Branch Rifle Club. (*Claymore*, June 1957.)

Biggar Branch Eighteenth Annual Dinner held in 1951. Brigadier-General R. M. Dudgeon, D.S.O., M.C., J.P., fourth from left, was guest of honour. (From *The Claymore*, May 1951.)

comfort of well-loved things around them in their own homes. The Women's Section are fully conscious of this, and their members generously undertake to visit and help old people in their homes where they make them happy and comfortable by doing the small chores like darning and mending, cleaning and tidying, reading to them, writing their letters and, above all, listening to their reminiscences of an older day. They have presented television sets to hospitals for their long-term patients ; they have sent regular Christmas presents to their own local lads serving overseas ; and they have helped to raise funds for their linked Legion branch. An organization whose members are prepared to do that sort of kindness to their neighbours must indeed be counted a valuable asset to the community.

There is one further aspect of their work which remains to be told, and it is one which is bound up with their hospital visiting, which has been mentioned earlier on. Some of the Women's Sections which are fortunate enough to be situated in seaside resorts have hit upon the happy idea of " adopting " disabled ex-Service men and women and giving them a seaside holiday in their own homes. Knowing how difficult and expensive seaside lodgings can be, one can only marvel at the kindly insight displayed by the Fairy Godmother Committee of the Section that first thought of it, and the selfless generosity of those who carry out the scheme.

The Women's Section very properly attracts the publicity it deserves, although some of the reporting is not always as accurate as they would like. For instance, one Women's Section president was said to have announced that " on Wednesday, 15th June, the Annual General Meeting will be hell " and later, that " the outing last Sunday was a hug success." Finally, there was the local paper's account of a Jumble Sale held by the Section which finished by saying " every member had brought something she no longer needed. Many members brought their husbands." Nevertheless, rising superior to such trivialities, the Women's Section now numbers 160 branches in seven areas with a membership of 8,000, and continues to play an essential part in the ever-widening scope of the Legion activities.

CHAPTER VII

BATTLEGROUNDS AND BATTLE HONOURS

" The labourer is worthy of his hire."

IT is probably true to say that more time and energy has been expended, and more Legion ink spilled since 1921 over the twin questions of Pensions and Employment than over any other two subjects. A completely documented volume could be written about them ; in fact, it might be easier to do so than to condense the history of this continuous and fluctuating battle, as the writer is bound to do, in this brief chapter. But even if it were easier to write, it would be less easy to understand as the reader would hardly be able to discern the shape of the wood for the multiplicity of the trees. The object now is to trace in outline and achievement the fortunes of this forty-year fight.

Of the millions who came back in 1919 to take off their uniforms and resume their interrupted lives, many were entitled to Pensions and Allowances of various categories, but did not know how to obtain them ; many had no employment to follow and were both unqualified and powerless to obtain it in a highly competitive world. The British Legion Scotland was founded in 1921 with the intention, duly stated in its Constitution, of assisting these returned fighters and their dependents in all their difficulties, in pension matters, in the relief of distress, in finding employment and in re-establishing them on their return. It found its own means to do this, developed its own technique, expanded its organization, and when the second tidal wave struck the country some twenty years later, it was ready with most of the answers. Here, then, is the outline of the Legion's strategy and tactics in this continuous campaign.

It must not be assumed, because of the Legion's constant attacks, that the Government was ever unsympathetic to the cause of the ex-Serviceman and his family. The Ministry of Pensions and the Ministry of Labour, the Unemployment Insurance Act, the Unemployment Assistance Board, with all their attendant machinery of regulations, were all empowered to deal with the Legion's cases. But it is a fact that regulations are framed to suit the majority, and there is a well-known Latin tag which runs " *De minimis non curat lex,*" and may be freely translated as " The rules don't cater for individuals." Mindful of this, the Legion's tactics on the pensions front were to help and guide the applications of those entitled under the regulations, and to cause these regulations to be amended so as to cover those who were *not* so entitled.

On the Employment front, the Legion's policy was to educate public opinion in the need for giving preference to ex-Servicemen seeking jobs, and to influence successive Governments and all Local Authorities to give *Statutory preference* to ex-Servicemen in all State [1] and local schemes for

---

[1] The King's Roll scheme by which firms guaranteed to employ a percentage of disabled men was one of the fruits of this policy, but the Legion pronounced it a failure by 1926.

employment. The pursuit of these lines, of course, meant the establishment and maintenance of friendly relationship with the appropriate Ministries. This was promptly done, and from the very formation of the Legion it was invited to send deputations to state its case to the Ministries, and to give evidence before Select and Departmental Committees. During the long course of its subsequent skirmishes and negotiations with the Ministries the Legion was ably assisted by its widespread membership among the professional ranks of lawyers, doctors and industrialists, and in both Houses of Parliament. Following the lead of their Founder, these gentlemen all gave their time and their services free in order to improve the lot of their brother officers and men ; and it is due to their persistence that the Legion won the " Battle Honours " described in this chapter.

The basis of all argument was the War Pensions Act of 1921—the instrument containing the regulations governing the issue of pensions in respect of service in the 1914-18 War—and it was the Legion's constant aim to see that the provisions of this Act and of the Royal Warrant on the same subject were sympathetically interpreted on behalf of disabled men and their families. Generally speaking, the Legion's activities had as their aim the constant amendment of the Act in accordance with changing conditions ; and this, in its turn, necessitated continual examination of all new legislature that might bear hardly on the Legion's members. By the time the Second World War broke out, its action had been so successful that its work mainly consisted of bringing individual cases within the orbit of the Pensions Scheme where these were not already covered. Of the many amendments to the War Pensions Act obtained by the Legion up to 1939, the following may be cited as " Battle Honours."

1. *The rates of pensions were permanently stabilized.*

2. *The majority of pensions awards had been made final.*

3. *Ex-Servicemen were allowed to submit claims at any time and not necessarily within seven years, as before.*

4. *Provision had been made for increased awards where disablement had become permanently and substantially worse.*

And though there might still be occasions when the Legion was forced to adopt a vigorous policy towards the Government, and obliged to take strong action through its branches (and even publicly) to secure amendments or alteration, by and large the Pensions Scheme worked satisfactorily, and the Legion's work was limited to helping the " special case " and the " hard luck story." Nevertheless, it would be true to say that by far the greater part of its work was that of assisting applicants for pensions in their inevitable battle by filling in their claim forms for them, and especially by helping them to obtain all the relevant supporting medical evidence. Cold print alone cannot convey the comfort and confidence engendered in its members by the Legion's successful endeavours in this field.

Nor can it convey the humour and the pathos (much of it unconscious) contained in some of the applications received at Headquarters. If Mr Connolly, the original Pensions Officer of the Legion, ever wrote his memoirs they would no doubt have included those pathetically comic descriptions of domestic circumstances, e.g., " My wife has no clothes and is being visited by the clergy," and " My wife is ill. She is in bed with the doctor," with which the applications were frequently embellished. It is a tribute to his sympathy and his hard work that the cause of the needy was so constantly

Photograph by courtesy of the "Peoples Journal" Dundee.

THE LEGION'S LUXURY HOTEL
Bradbury, North Berwick

This luxury hotel at boarding-house prices has first-class cooking, T.V., putting and bowling greens, and is only three minutes' walk from the beach.

Top charge is £1 a day. People wanting to go there don't have to be members of the Legion as long as they are ex-Service personnel.

Priority is given to those who have been off work through illness and are convalescing.

Ex-Service applications for those who cannot afford the full amount are also considered, as are those for holidays only (at full charge). The application forms are such that private details can be kept confidential.

Write to :—

BRITISH LEGION SCOTLAND,
23 DRUMSHEUGH GARDENS,
EDINBURGH, 3.

upheld and justice so often obtained. But pension successes did not die with Mr Connolly, for Mr Wood and later Major Russell Thompson, the present Pensions Officer, consolidated his work. The figures are for Head-quarters only, and do not include the excellent attainments of the areas and branches.[1] Figures only faintly convey the real significance of the benefits gained for ex-Servicemen ; but a few at least deserve to be given in order to show the magnitude of the work that was done. The bare facts, then, are that throughout the Legion about a million and a half cases were dealt with ; over ten thousand cases had been represented at the Pensions Appeal Tribunals ; the total amount of arrears secured for ex-Servicemen was one million pounds ; and the yearly value of the pensions was one and a quarter million. These figures may well be allowed to speak for themselves.

On the " Employment Front " the struggle continued, grim and un-relenting, right up to 1937 when the mounting tide of rearmament began to lower the total of the unemployed. This was a problem which concerned not only the Legion (and therefore ex-Servicemen), but in fact the manhood of the entire nation. For when Great Britain slid off the gold standard in 1931, unemployment figures reached a new height and the prospects for many a home were bleak indeed. But—and here was the root of the matter as far as the Legion was concerned—the queues at the Labour Exchanges now included a new generation of men, too young to fight in the war, but young enough to be preferred in the labour market to those who had. Thus the ageing ex-soldier was confronted by another serious obstacle in his search for work. This fresh challenge was promptly accepted by the Legion, whose representatives now ceased to rely on the persuasion line of policy originally adopted. The Legion now began to try its own hand at finding employment for its members, and although this could never be attempted on a large scale, the idea was successful in its own way. Apart from its own job-finding organization which aimed at suiting both employer and employee, the Poppy Factory was founded and the Car Park Attendants' Scheme initiated, small but useful ventures which, incidentally, have stood the test of time. Ephemeral chances such as employing a few hundred men at the Glasgow Exhibition of 1938, and in the Recruiting Offices in 1939, were eagerly seized as they presented themselves. Meanwhile Occupational Centres had been established at various places in the kingdom, and the Legion took early opportunity to support these wherever possible, and to send its members to them in order to keep fit in body and alert in mind whilst temporarily unemployed. But all these schemes were drops in the ocean of a national disaster, from which the Legion sought by every con-stitutional means to rescue the ex-Servicemen. It could alleviate the pain, but could not cure it.

In this protracted conflict, the Legion's first and most important task was to follow with a vigilant eye the development and application of the Unemployment Insurance Acts and the Unemployment Assistance Board Regulations. In particular it was concerned about the unfair application of the Means Test to the War Pensioner, maintaining strongly that no disability pension should be taken into account when assessing the applicant's total income. So, while many areas and branches set up their own Relief Councils for helping own local comrades, the Legion campaigned on a high level against the particular evil of the Means Test, and the dishonourable fact that ex-Servicemen should have to apply to their Parish Council for

[1] See Graph, page 117.

Photograph by courtesy of "Glen Pictorials," Stranraer.

H.R.H. The Duchess of Gloucester reviewing the Parade of ex-Servicemen during her 1953 visit to Stranraer. (From *The Claymore*, December 1953.)

Photograph by courtesy of "Edinburgh Evening News."

After a Pilgrimage to Holland in 1955 to visit the graves of their fathers, who were killed in the war, this picture was taken of four Scots children returning to their homes, at the Waverley Station, Edinburgh, after arrival from London. (From *The Claymore* July 1955.)

relief instead of to a Labour Exchange. Often acting in close co-operation with the Legion in England, these two issues were fought throughout the dark years of the early thirties ; but while the Parish Relief problem was habitually refused revision by the responsible Minister, the Means Test campaign was rather more successful, and the following " Battle Honours " fall to be recorded. In 1932, a joint Anglo-Scottish Legion deputation was received by the Minister of Labour, who made two valuable proposals. These were :

    (i) That the Legion should submit evidence and facts to the Royal Commission on Unemployment Insurance which might introduce favouring clauses affecting ex-Servicemen in the future,

and

    (ii) That the British Legion would be recognized as a kind of " Court of Investigation " regarding cases of harsh treatment by Public Assistance Committees which might be brought to its notice.

Next year, following pressure by the Legion, the Government decided that up to 50% of a disability pension should be discounted in connection with the Means Test ; and as the direct result of further representations in 1934, it was ruled that the first £1 of a disability pension should be disregarded. These valuable improvements were rightly regarded as " Battle Honours," while at the same time it was agreed by the Annual Conference that the Legion should continue to exert pressure on this subject by every constitutional means.

Armed with its mandate from the Ministry of Labour to act as a " Court of Investigation," the Legion continued vigilantly to scrutinize all cases of hardship brought to its notice, and in one case at least it went as far as to take legal action to uphold the rights of a member. The case, as a sample of a " Battle Honour," is worth recording in outline. It arose out of a claim for relief by an Aberdeenshire man called Duncan which was refused by the Public Assistance Committee of the County Council. As he was an ex-Serviceman, one hundred per cent disabled, unfit for work, and married with five children too young to work, the Legion took up his cause. An appeal was made to the Sheriff who gave judgment in the man's favour ; but the County Council appealed against this judgment and the case was heard in the Court of Session, where their Lordships upheld the County Council. Notwithstanding this setback, the National Council, with legal advice, took the case to the House of Lords and won it, thus vindicating the position of the British Legion. It is only fair to add that the leading parts in this successful legal battle were taken on the Legion's behalf by Mr J. C. M. Guy, M.C., M.P. and Mr J. Stevenson, K.C.[1]

And still the general engagement against Unemployment continued relentlessly by constitutional methods until at the Annual Conference in 1936 the subject was bracketed with Pensions in a Resolution to petition the Government to establish a Committee of Inquiry into

"The present condition of all ex-Servicemen who fought in the late War and also their dependents who are suffering from physical and financial stress due to lack of Pension and Employment."

Not unnaturally, the Ministry of Pensions refused to take action on a Resolution couched in such general terms, so the National Council set up

[1] Later Lord Stevenson.

Blended and Bottled by

ROBERT McNISH & CO. LTD.

45 Washington Street, Glasgow C.3

its special Committee of Inquiry in order to produce the necessary facts and information for the Minister. To obtain these, a " Questionnaire " was drawn up and sent to all areas and branches. But though much trouble and care had gone into the preparation of this document, it would seem that insufficient thought had been given to the form in which the Legion's case was presented. Although the Legion in England was acting on the same lines, and took concerted action by forming a joint deputation with Scotland in 1938 which was received by the Prime Minister himself, the Government answer was, in brief, that no grounds for establishing a Committee of Inquiry had been shown. Of this event, another historian [1] has written :

> " The problem of the ageing ex-Serviceman was a real and tragic one and demanded the Legion's attention, but it merited more thought and investigation as a prelude to action."

Seen from a distance of nearly twenty years, that may indeed be a fair commentary. At any rate, the Prime Minister's reply to this truly representative delegation virtually closed the door to further negotiations on these lines ; and shortly afterwards the advent of a Second World War presented the Legion's organization with other and wider responsibilities.

The unemployment problem now vanished from the picture, but Pensions at once became a pressing matter since an entirely new pensionable class was enrolling as members. But the War found the Legion ready for its task, and its watchdogs were vigilant as ever to scrutinize the implications of the new Pensions Instruments of September 1939. These instruments laid down that a pension should be paid only in respect of disablement certified to be directly attributable to, or materially aggravated by, war service ; or death similarly certified. These conditions of course implied the existence of evidence and a reasonably high standard of proof, and the Legion was not slow to join issue with the Ministry and press for modifications. It took some time, but a notable success was obtained in 1943 when the Government decided on a far-reaching alteration of the rules, the effect of which was that the applicant was no longer obliged to prove his case ; he was given the benefit of any doubt ; and the Ministry, unless it *was* prepared to award a pension, was obliged to prove that such an award ought *not* to be made. This entirely altered the conception of pension entitlement, and there can be no doubt that the benefit to ex-Servicemen was considerable. There was an immediate increase in the number of pensions awarded, and the broader basis of entitlement enabled many thousands of claims to be admitted both during and after the war. There were further concessions, too, in that year of 1943, and perhaps the most important was the raising of the basic rate of pension from 32s. 6d. for the 1939 War pensioners to 40s. (the 100% disablement rate of 1918). During the years that followed the war this rate was gradually raised until it reached 85s., where it stands to-day.

Other " Battle Honours " gained during and since the war include the following :—

> *An automatic entitlement to allowances for wife and children in contrast to the requirement that marriage must have taken place before disablement.*

> *An Unemployability Supplement, now 55s. a week. There was no comparable allowance in the past.*

> *Increase in the rate of Constant Attendance Allowance.*

---

[1] Graham Wotton, *The Official History of the British Legion*, page 213.

Introduction of Comforts Allowance.

Age Supplement for pensioners of sixty-five years or over in receipt of a pension assessed at 40% or more.

Slightly improved allowances for children.

An allowance for lowered standard of occupation.

The 1914-18 War widows, who were granted pension in 1946-47, i.e., those widows who had married after the pensioner received his disablement and the death of the pensioner occurred on or after 3rd September 1939— received an important improvement.

A Rent Allowance for widows with qualifying children.

Supplements for war widows aged seventy years or over.

But the Legion is not complacent, and has certainly not allowed matters to rest there. There are still far too many anomalies in the operation of Pensions and Allowances which it would like to see abolished, and it has never ceased to represent these, on behalf of its members, to successive Governments. For instance, it would like to see a substantial increase in the present rate of war pensions and war widows' pensions ; the right of independent appeal ; and a greater disregard of disability pensions and war widows' pensions by National Assistance Boards. But Governments are notoriously hard to move ; and though not unfavourably inclined towards those who have served our country, they are not unduly influenced by their claims. So far the Legion has achieved its early objectives ; but early in 1959 it launched a new offensive. Co-operating with thirty other ex-Service Organizations, it was represented on a deputation which interviewed the Minister of Pensions and National Insurance and put forward nine points for his consideration. There were almost immediate results. First the Government introduced an Age Supplement of 10s. per week to war widows of seventy years of age or over, and then the National Assistance Board decided to disregard the first 10s. 6d. a week of a war widow's pension. Though it is dangerous to prophesy, one cannot help feeling that such a responsible expression of public feeling will result in even greater concessions.

The Second World War threw up two new problems for the British Legion to shoulder, and the first of these appeared as an entirely new word —Resettlement. It was not enough to find employment for the returning warrior : in many cases he heeded a helping hand to start a new life in new surroundings. The war had destroyed houses, shifted industries and scattered whole families, and men and women were facing with what fortitude they might the formidable task of building their lives anew. Often this required not only material but spiritual resources, and where the Legion was able to help it did so with practical aid. A National Resettlement Committee was formed to deal with the multiplicity of cases on which they were invited to advise, and its counterpart was to be found in every area in Scotland. Achievements in this field of endeavour are difficult to list because of the diverse nature of the problems. By far the largest of these, at any rate in the years immediately following the war, was housing. Here the Committee was forced to act in an advisory capacity because it was found that representations to Local Authorities seldom produced anything more than a vague reply to the effect that the applicant " still had a long time to wait," though in a few cases they were followed by the speedy allocation of a house.

Perhaps the best work done on this thorny subject was the provision of sound advice based on an extensive knowledge of the rules. Nor was this

the only subject on which advice was sought. The following list shows *some* of the others :—

Business Loans and Problems.
Change of Employment.
Education.
Hire Purchase.
Homes for Old People.
Income Tax.
Medals.
National Service Grants.
Redundancy.
Reinstatement, etc., etc.

It is hard to draw an accurate line which will divide Resettlement from Employment on one side, and Welfare on the other. Nor, in fact, would it be necessary to do so as far as the beneficiaries were concerned. They came for advice and help on their own problems, and that was what they got. As far as the Legion was concerned it was " just another part of the service " (to borrow the slogan of a well-known firm). Those who provide that knowledgeable advice, generally the Legion's legal friends, prefer to remain anonymous. But those at the receiving end know them with gratitude : the ex-Seaforth who obtained compensation for an accident at work ; the wife of an ex-Navy man who obtained compensation for an injury sustained over ten years ago ; the ex-Royal Scots bandsman who was enabled to prove that he lost his private saxophone by enemy action in Hong Kong and was accordingly compensated and helped to take up his former trade as a musician. These are but three examples from many thousands who have benefited by the Legion's staff and legal and medical friends—and who will not forget them.

The other word generated by the Second World War was Welfare. True, it was hardly a new word for the Legion. Ever since 1921 each branch had worked and cared for its members and their families ; each Women's Section had been active in visiting the old and the sick in home or hospital ; and both men and women had been quick to bring deserving cases to the notice of the existing Welfare Organizations.

The Legion in England had already begun to organize annual Pilgrimages to the War Graves in France and Flanders in which families from Scotland were invited to participate ; and after the Second World War they greatly enlarged the scope of these with a further resulting benefit to Scotland also.

But, in addition to the close liaison with the various Welfare Organizations in Scotland, the Legion felt that it ought to have a welfare project of its own. Discussion eventually hatched out the idea of a Holiday Home where those in need of rest and recuperation could stay in the best of comfort at a price they could well afford. The development of this idea was helped a stage further by the unexpected gift to the Legion of a suitable house. Colonel R. G. Sillars presented his own home, " Ardgare," on the shores of the Gareloch for use as a Holiday Home, and it was formally opened in 1949.[1] In the same year the Legion bought, with financial assistance from the Earl Haig Fund, a modern hotel at North Berwick called " Bradbury," and this has been successfully run as a Holiday-cum-Convalescent Home for ten years. The value of it is attested by the many letters, some of which have appeared from time to time in *The Claymore*, but one suspects that

[1] It has since been sold.

Photograph by courtesy " Kelso Chronicle and Mail."

The Standards on parade at the 1955 Founder's Day Service at Dryburgh Abbey.
(From *The Claymore*, August 1955.)

Photograph by courtesy of A. Grier, 29 Bridge Street, Musselburgh.

Musselburgh Branch's newly-formed Football Team wearing their new Legion colours
—blue shirts with Legion badge and blue stockings. The collars and cuffs and stocking
tops are of gold to match. (From *The Claymore*, February 1955.)

78

there are many equally grateful guests who do not put pen to paper ! All in all, it is a fine example of private enterprise, and a fulfilment of the Legion's saying " We give service *after* service."

This slogan is once again assuming a new importance in connection with the employment of those officers and men who are now leaving the Services in the course of the reduction in strength of the Armed Forces. Though full employment awaited those who were discharged in the ordinary way after their service contract, this extra reduction will mean that a very large number of able men between forty and fifty years old will be thrown on the labour market at a difficult time in their lives. But the Legion is alive to this problem ; it has fought a similar battle in the past, and is prepared to do so again in the changed circumstances. All its resources are mobilized, and it is vigorously assisting in the work of the " Job Finder," a special appointment made by the Earl Haig Fund (Scotland). The Government has done what it can for these men, and has not been inconsiderate ; but the Legion will, as ever, do all in its power to help them in their search for a prolonged life of service. And in doing so, it will be greatly aided by public opinion.

Cars
for all ranks
at Wylie & Lochhead

CHAPTER VIII

REMEMBRANCE

"O Valiant hearts, who to your glory came
Through dust of conflict and through battle flame."

IF you were to ask the average young man of under twenty-five years what he knows about the British Legion, he would probably answer rather vaguely : " It's the men who fought in ' The War.' " And if you were to press your point and say " Yes—but what do they do ? " he would almost certainly reply, " Well, they have a thing called Remembrance Day and lay a wreath of poppies on the War Memorial." That public act of Remembrance of comrades who fell in two world wars is the unique gesture that the Legion has made its own ; yet the young man could not have told you why the poppy was chosen for the wreath, nor what was its particular significance. But his father had known.

It was during the First World War that the profusion of poppies growing in the devastated areas of Flanders was noticed by those engaged in the conflict. More particularly it was observed that they were growing wild in all the places where our dead lay buried, and men began to associate this little flower with their fallen Comrades. But it was given a wider and more cosmopolitan significance by the publication in *Punch* of the following poem, early in 1915 :

IN FLANDERS' FIELDS [1]

In Flanders' fields the poppies blow
Between the crosses, row on row,
That mark our place, and in the sky
The larks, still bravely singing, fly
Scarce heard amid the guns below.

We are the Dead.   Short days ago
We lived, felt dawn, saw sunsets glow,
Loved and were loved, and now we lie
In Flanders' fields.

Take up our quarrel with the foe ;
To you, from failing hands, we throw
The torch ; be yours to hold it high.
If ye break faith with us who die
We shall not sleep, though poppies grow
In Flanders' fields.

Though published anonymously (as was the *Punch* custom with all except its regular contributors) the poem was in fact written by a Canadian Colonel called John McRae of McGill University while he was serving as a Medical Officer with the Canadian contingent in the Second Battle of Ypres. It made a wide appeal to many hearts—and not only on this side of the

---

[1] Reprinted by kind permission of *Punch*.

Atlantic. One of those on whom it made a profound impression was an American lady called Miss Moina Michael ; and as soon as the war was over she persuaded American ex-Servicemen to adopt the poppy as their emblem. These poppies were manufactured by an organization in the devastated areas of France by women, for the benefit of the children, and then shipped to the United States. It is sad to have to record that Colonel McRae did not survive to see this first adoption of the poppy emblem which his timely poem had inspired.

That was the first distant move towards what we now have established as " Poppy Day." Contact with the British Legion was first made in 1921 when a lady connected with the French organization mentioned above came over to London and interested British Legion officials there in the bulk purchase of poppies ; and the first, hurriedly improvised Poppy Day collection was held on 11th November 1921, the third anniversary of the Armistice. The growth of this National Day is a matter of history, and the monies raised annually by the distribution of the poppy emblem and paid into Earl Haig's Fund have been the sinews which have enabled the relief of distress among countless war veterans and their dependents to be organized as it is to-day. It was that Fund—and nothing else—that financed the young and spreading movement from its inception. No grant from the Government has ever been received.

Poppy Day is, and always has been, a vast co-operative and voluntary effort by men, women and children of every town and village throughout the country which has developed into a National Day worth, over the years, many millions of pounds to the cause of the ex-Serviceman.

As the idea of Poppy Day captured the public's imagination, the law of supply and demand indicated that the poppies and wreaths might well be manufactured in this country. The Legion in England established a Factory at Richmond (Surrey). In 1926 Lady Haig, with an initial grant from the Earl Haig Fund in Scotland, started a small Factory under its own council and management with the aim of manufacturing poppies, and at the same time employing disabled ex-Servicemen on the work. It still stands on its original site in the Canongate of Edinburgh but, as with all successful enterprises, it has developed and widened its field of activities. Besides the making of all the poppies and wreaths required in Scotland, other crafts were taught and mastered at the Factory so that a shop became a necessity to display and sell the resulting products. Premises at 33 George Street, Edinburgh, were acquired where a representative stock of the various articles made at the Factory could be shown and sold to the public. Mindful of the well-known slogan " It pays to advertise," the Factory soon took to the idea of having stalls at all the big shows and exhibitions, displaying their activities to a larger world and, as a direct result, keeping over 80 disabled men in regular work. And that, as a contribution to the perennial problem of unemployment, was significant.

At this point the writer may, with justice, be accused of " putting the cart before the horse " in that only a brief reference has been made to the Earl Haig Fund as it exists in Scotland, and its relationship to the British Legion Scotland. The Field-Marshal issued in 1921 an " Appeal " under his own name for ex-Service men and women and their dependents of all ranks who had served in the war. This Appeal was launched and operated originally by the existing Officers' Association on both sides of the Border, and the money subscribed was to be divided proportionately between officers and men.

THE STEEL TUBE AGE

The artist's impression shows S & L steel pipes supplied for the North of Scotland Hydro-Electric Board's Tummel Garry Scheme.

The pipes have an outside diameter of $30\frac{3}{4}$ inches and are $\frac{5}{16}$ inch thick. They have sleeve joints for welding, with a Vulcan expansion joint between each pair of anchors.

The pipeline is to convey compensation water from Errochty Dam, which can be seen in the illustration, to a power station near Trinafour.

Consulting Engineers: Sir Alexander Gibb & Partners

STEWARTS AND LLOYDS LIMITED

GLASGOW · BIRMINGHAM · LONDON

Registered Office: 41 OSWALD STREET, P.O. BOX 5, GLASGOW, C.1

S&L

In England, however, the Association preferred, after they obtained a Royal Charter, not to handle money for other ranks, and therefore they passed the responsibility for organizing the Poppy Day Appeal to the British Legion. In Scotland the position was different. In response to requests from influential subscribers and by general agreement, the organization of the Appeal, the collection and distribution of the money, was left in the hands of The Officers' Association represented by the Scottish branch in Edinburgh and by the South-Western branch in Glasgow.

The name of Earl Haig Fund was added as a supplementary title, and this position continued until 1954, the money allocated to Other Ranks being treated as held " in trust."

Thus the segregation of the benevolent side of the work to the Earl Haig Fund left the Legion responsible for general welfare, with particular emphasis on Pensions and Resettlement problems, a charge which by its devoted voluntary work throughout Scotland it has ably fulfilled.

In 1954 the Officers' Association (Scottish Branch) decided to constitute The Earl Haig Fund (Scotland) with a separate Constitution and to hand over to it the custody of all funds held for Other Ranks and the organizing of the Poppy Day collection.

The link between the British Legion Scotland and the Earl Haig Fund was consolidated by including in the Council of the former the President and Chairman of the Legion (ex-officio) and four nominated members.

The British Legion Scotland as a gesture, hands over to the Earl Haig Fund (Scotland) its share in the Overseas Poppy Day Collection.

To-day the Earl Haig Fund (Scotland) operates in two Areas throughout Scotland under a Central Council with Headquarters in Edinburgh, but for administrative purposes has established the "North, South and East" and the "Glasgow and South-West" Areas. The Fund was registered as a charity in 1921, and after the Second World War started was registered under the War Charities Act, and its scope was extended to include a new generation of fighters. It is now helping the sons of that generation, those who have fought since 1945 in any of the scattered theatres of war such as Korea, Kenya, Cyprus and Malaya, and thus maintains the purpose for which it was formed nearly forty years ago.

The great public Day of Remembrance, of course, had its origin in the Commemoration of the Armistice of 1918. When that instrument came into effect at 11 o'clock on the morning of the 11th November, the noise of gunfire which had filled men's days and nights for nearly five years was suddenly stilled. To those at the front this dramatic silence seemed to have an almost divine quality that touched their hearts. They never forgot it—nor did the Nations of the World. In every civilised country, by official decree, a silence of two minutes was observed every year on this date and at this hour. All movement ceased, all noise was hushed, and life itself appeared suspended for those hundred and twenty seconds in which the fallen were reverently remembered. It was a deeply moving event, and Lawrence Binyon's lines, befitting the occasion, were known and quoted by the English-speaking world :

> " They shall not grow old, as we that are left grow old :
> Age shall not weary them, nor the years condemn.
> At the going down of the sun and in the morning
> We will remember them."

Photograph by courtesy of Norwood Inglis, 18 Regent Terrace, Edinburgh.

Sorting out the thousands of forecasts for the 1956 Competition of Skill on the Derby. The photograph shows the band of willing volunteers working late into the night in the Boardroom at Legion Headquarters. (From *The Claymore*, July 1956.)

Photograph by courtesy of Day's, Photographer, 19 High Street, North Berwick.

The Countess of Haddington receives a bouquet from Miss Jane McAlpine after opening the 1957 British Legion Fête at North Berwick. (From *The Claymore*, November 1957.)

The National Act of Remembrance took place with proper pomp and circumstance, first at the Mercat Cross, and later at the Stone of Remembrance outside the City Chambers of Edinburgh ; but in every town and village of Scotland also the poppies were being sold, the wreaths laid on the War Memorials, the two minutes of silence thoughtfully observed. And in every church in the land, on the Sunday nearest to Armistice Day, designated " Armistice Sunday," the theme of the Service was that of Sacrifice, and the offerings were devoted to Earl Haig's Fund so that the living as well as the dead should not be forgotten. Nor was that all ; for in the large cities and towns, men and women would meet again in the evening, in their own gathering places, to remember their dead and to re-dedicate their lives amid a " cloud of witnesses."

Twenty-one years later another and greater conflict was waged by another and younger generation, whose claim to Remembrance is as great as their fathers'. This war did not cease as dramatically as did the first : three widely separated months saw the end of it in the West and in the East, and the sudden lull of the " Armistice " was no longer relevant. But there was the same deep thankfulness in the hearts of men, women and children, and the same wish to give thanks for deliverance and pay homage to sacrifice. And so the vital " Two Minutes' Silence " became merged into the religious service which was still universally held on the same November Sunday. Re-christened " Remembrance Day," it thenceforward commemorated the dead of two wars, with the poppy still silently appealing from an older to a younger world. And the strength of its appeal to all may be seen in the little crosses, each crowned with a poppy and planted year by year not only in the " Field of Remembrance " outside Westminster Abbey, but in many a place in Scotland.

And, as this great public act of Remembering the dead is formally finished by the musical expression of loyalty to the Crown, each member of the Legion must echo in his heart the words of the poet[1] who wrote of his own Regiment some seventy years ago.

> " God Save the Queen ! " we living sing,
>   From height to height 'tis heard ;
> And with the rest your voices ring,
>   Lads of the Fifty-third.
>
> Oh God will save her, fear you not :
>   Be you the men you've been,
> Get you the sons your fathers got,
>   And God will save the Queen."

[1] A. E. Housman : " A Shropshire Lad."

SCOTLAND

In Appreciation of our

Very Cordial Relationship

with Officials and Members

throughout Scotland

ROBERT DEUCHAR
LIMITED

DUDDINGSTON BREWERY

EDINBURGH 9

APPENDIX A

THE CONSTITUTION OF THE BRITISH LEGION SCOTLAND

(*From* 1950 *Revised Issue*)

RULE 1—TITLE

(*a*) The title of the Organisation shall be "THE BRITISH LEGION SCOTLAND," and it is hereinafter referred to as " The Legion."

(*b*) The Head Office of the Legion shall be in Edinburgh.

RULE 2—PRINCIPLES AND POLICY

(*a*) The Legion shall be democratic, non-sectarian, and not affiliated to or connected directly or indirectly with any Political Party or Political Organisation.

(*b*) The Legion has been created to preserve the spirit of fellowship and service to others formed by all ranks and to maintain, in a strong, stimulating, united and democratic comradeship all those who have served in His Majesty's Armed Forces, or any Auxiliary Forces, and others defined as eligible for membership under Rule 7 (hereinafter referred to as " Ex-Service Men and Women "), so that neither their efforts nor their interests shall be forgotten ; that their welfare and that of the dependents of the fallen may be safeguarded ; and that just and equitable treatment shall be secured to them in respect of the difficulties caused in their lives as a result of their services.

(*c*) The Legion exists to perpetuate in the civil life of the Empire and the World the principles for which the Nation stands ; to inculcate a sense of loyalty to the Crown, Community, State and Nation ; to promote unity amongst all classes ; to make right the master of might ; to secure peace and goodwill on earth ; to safeguard and transmit to posterity the principles of justice, freedom and democracy, and to consecrate and sanctify comradeship by devotion to mutual service and helpfulness.

RULE 3—AIMS AND OBJECTS

(*a*) To bring about the co-operation of all ex-Service men and women, and to establish Branches of the Legion.

(*b*) To perpetuate the memory of those who died in the service of their country.

(*c*) To educate public opinion to the view that the maintenance of the disabled and the welfare of ex-Service men and women and their dependents is a national duty.

(*d*) To obtain public recognition for the principle that ex-Service men and women, in accordance with their qualifications, are entitled to just and equitable treatment in all matters relating to the finding or provision of employment.

(*e*) To establish or support by financial or other means, including subscriptions for shares, suitable undertakings for the training and/or employment or otherwise for the benefit of ex-Service men and women, whether such undertakings shall be situate in Great Britain and Northern Ireland, or in the Dominions or Possessions Overseas or elsewhere, and to do all that may be necessary or requisite to enable ex-Service men and women or their dependents to take advantage of the opportunities offered by such undertakings.

(*f*) To assist ex-Service men and women to secure not less than the recognised standard rate of wages in accordance with their ability.

(*g*) To assist ex-Service men and women and the widows, children and dependents of those who have served in matters relating to pensions, allowances, grants, war gratuities, resettlement and rehabilitation.

The St. Andrews Dinner. Lieut.-Colonel Sir J. Reginald N. Graham, Bart., V.C., O.B.E., Earl Haig Fund (Scotland) is seen sitting on left beside Mr Norman King, Branch and Area Chairman. (From *The Claymore*, April 1959.)

Photograph by courtesy of " The Scotsman."

The first trial of strength in the British Legion International Bowls Tournament for the " Dumfries " Cup, in Edinburgh in 1948, between England and Scotland. Mr Webb, for England, plays the first wood.

(*h*) To promote the welfare of the women and children left by those who have fallen in His Majesty's service, and to arrange for them to visit the graves of relatives killed in war.

(*i*) To promote representation of the needs of ex-Service men and women, and their dependents, and of the widows and dependents of those who have served to or in Parliament, and to or on public bodies whose functions are defined by Act of Parliament or Order in Council.

(*j*) To advise serving men and women in connection with their return to civil life and promote the interests of their dependents while they are serving, except in so far as concerns their discipline, privileges and emoluments in money or kind under the Regulations in force for the time being of His Majesty's Naval, Military, or Air Forces respectively.

(*k*) To promote and support schemes for the education of ex-Service men and women and their children.

(*l*) To solicit and receive subscriptions and gifts of all kinds, whether absolute or conditional, for the objects of the Legion, and to obtain money for such objects by the organisation of entertainments, the sale of badges, or by any other legal means, and for such purposes to advertise the Legion by any legal method that may commend itself to the National Executive Council, and in particular by the publication and sale of a Legion Journal.

(*m*) To raise and co-ordinate funds for the purpose of assisting ex-Service men and women and their dependents, and to combine and/or co-operate with, take over, amalgamate with, or absorb any other Society having objects which are included in the objects of the Legion.

(*n*) To see that all moneys raised or contributed from any source for the welfare of ex-Service men and women or their dependents, or the widows, children and dependents of Service men killed in war, are utilised for that purpose and not devoted to any other (provided always that reasonable administrative expenses properly incurred in promoting the objects of the Legion shall be deemed to be included in that purpose), and to apply and dispose of the capital and income of the moneys and other property, whether heritable or moveable, from time to time vested in or belonging to the Legion for and towards the proper and effective carrying out of the aforesaid or similar objects, or any of them, and generally to do all things necessary or expedient for the proper and effective carrying out of any of the aforesaid or similar objects.

Provided always that any property, heritable or moveable, at any time or times taken over or raised by the Legion, or transferred, given, or contributed to the Legion subject to or upon any condition special trust or trusts shall be held and applied by the Legion upon and to such condition, special trust or trusts as may be applicable to the same and not otherwise, and shall be kept separate and apart from any other funds of the Legion.

OFFICE BEARERS 1959

Courtesy of Drummond Young, Edinburgh.

PRESIDENT

General SIR THOMAS RIDDELL-WEBSTER,
G.C.B., D.S.O., D.L.

CHAIRMAN

Mr T. Matheson, O.B.E., J.P.

Courtesy of Drummond Young, Edinburgh.

VICE-CHAIRMAN

Admiral of the Fleet
SIR RHODERICK MCGRIGOR,
G.C.B., D.S.O.

Courtesy of A. J. B. Strachan, Aberdeen.

HON. TREASURER

Major G. C. PATTERSON, C.A.

APPENDIX B

OFFICE BEARERS AT DATE OF PUBLICATION

President
General SIR T. S. RIDDELL-WEBSTER, G.C.B., D.S.O., D.L.

Chairman
Mr T. MATHESON, O.B.E., J.P.

Vice-Chairman
Admiral of the Fleet SIR RHODERICK McGRIGOR, G.C.B., D.S.O.

Hon. Treasurer
Major G. C. PATTERSON, C.A.

NATIONAL EXECUTIVE COUNCIL

Mr A. ANDERSON.
Mr J. ANDERSON.

Lieut.-Colonel The Hon. DAVID A. BALFOUR, T.D.
Mr NORMAN BARRON.
Mr F. J. BEHAN.
Mr ALAN M. BROWN.
Mr R. BROWN, M.B.E., M.A.

Captain D. L. CARSWELL.

Mr KENNETH DAVIDSON.
Captain D. G. DINGWALL-MAIN.
Captain W. A. DRUMMOND.
Mr C. J. DUGUID.

Mr H. FALCONER.

Lieut.-Colonel SIR J. R. N. GRAHAM, Bart., V.C., O.B.E.
Captain ALEX. GRAY.
Lieut.-Colonel R. GRIMSHAW, O.B.E., J.P.

Mr A. HAMILTON.
Mr T. C. HAMILTON, M.B.E., J.P.

Major R. HARGREAVES, M.B.E.
Mr F. W. C. HAY.
Major A. HUME.

Mr C. A. KENT.
Mr CHAS. KING.
Mr NORMAN R. KING.

Bailie R. LEISHMAN.
Lieut.-Colonel R. N. LEVITT, M.B.E., T.D.

Lieut.-Colonel A. MACDONALD.
Mr L. MACKINNON.
Lieut.-Colonel NORMAN MACLEOD, C.M.G., C.B.E., D.S.O., D.L., J.P.
Mr R. MACLEOD.
Coun. A. M. McKILLOP, D.A., A.R.I.B.A.
Colonel D. McCORQUODALE, O.B.E.
Mr M. McGEOCH, D.C.M.
Mr G. McMAHON.
Major JOHN MITCHELL, C.B.E., T.D.

Mr WM. MITCHELL.
Lieut.-Colonel D. W. M. MORRISON, O.B.E., M.C., T.D., J.P.
Lieut.-Colonel T. H. M. MURRAY, M.B.E.

Mr JAMES NORMAN.

Mr A. J. C. PROVAN, J.P.

Mr J. RAMAGE, D.A. (EDIN).
Captain JAMES ROBB, M.M.

Dr. D. STEWART, O.B.E., T.D.
Mr A. S. STUART, M.B.E.

Mr A. THOMSON.
Captain T. TOMLINSON.

Mr J. L. SCOTT VEITCH, C.A.

Major T. M. WEDDERBURN, T.D., W.S., C.A. (Hon. Legal Adviser).
Mr M. M. WILKIE.

Note.—Major-General SIR AYMER MAXWELL, C.B.E., M.C., D.L. is a Life Member of the N.E.C. under Rule 10 (a) of the Constitution.

General Secretary
Colonel C. S. MacLEOD OF GLENDALE, T.D.

The British Legion Scotland is represented by N.E.C. Members and others on the following outside Committees—Scottish National Institution for War Blinded; National Playing Fields Association; Scottish Command T.A. Recruiting Committee; British Commonwealth Ex-Services League; Army Benevolent Fund—Scottish Grants Sub-Committee; Scottish Veterans' Garden City Association; Scottish National War Memorial; Scottish Council of Physical Recreation; Astley Ainslie, Edenhall and Associated Hospitals Board of Management; South-Eastern Regional Hospitals Board; and the Scottish Council of Social Service (Village Halls Committee).

WOMEN'S SECTION

President
THE COUNTESS OF HADDINGTON.

Chairman
MRS C. RORIE, B.E.M.

General Secretary & Treasurer
MRS J. B. MORTON.

Pack up your Guinness
in your old kitbag

GUINNESS
is worth while

G.E.3098.B

APPENDIX C

TABLE OF ANNUAL CONFERENCES AND CHAIRMEN

Year.	Place.	Chairman.
1921	Edinburgh	Colonel SIR W. S. DICK-CUNYNGHAM, Bart.
1922	Edinburgh	Mr ANDREW YOUNG, J.P., F.E.I.S.
1923	Glasgow	Captain J. L. CUMMING.
1924	Aberdeen	
1925	Kirkcaldy	
1926	Hamilton	LORD GLENTANAR., D.L.
1927	Dundee	
1928	Dumfries	
1929	Edinburgh	Mr J. GEDDES (*Vice-Chairman*).
1930	Kilmarnock	
1931	Inverness	
1932	Dunfermline	
1933	Rothesay	
1934	Edinburgh	THE EARL OF HADDINGTON, K.T., M.C., T.D.
	(*Special Conference* re "*Means Test*" *as applied to War Pensioners*)	
1934	Montrose	
1935	Peebles	
1936	Troon	
1937	Edinburgh	
	(*Special Conference* re *International Co-operation between ex-Servicemen*)	Lieut.-Colonel THE EARL OF AIRLIE, K.T., K.C.V.O., M.C.
1937	St. Andrews	
1938	Crieff	
1939	Aberdeen	
1940	(Cancelled because of War)	
1941	Edinburgh	
1942	Edinburgh	
1943	Edinburgh	Colonel W. MARTIN KAY, C.M.G., C.B.E., T.D., D.L.
1944	(Cancelled because of Government request re rail traffic)	(National Vice-Chairman, whilst Chairman was on active service.)
1945	Edinburgh	
1946	Edinburgh	Lieut.-Colonel THE EARL OF AIRLIE, K.T., G.C.V.O., M.C.
1946	Edinburgh	
	(*Special Conference for Revision of Constitution*)	
1947	Inverness	
1948	Dunoon	Major-General SIR JAMES SYME DREW, K.B.E., C.B., D.S.O., M.C., D.L.
1949	Dundee	
1950	Peebles	
1951	Glasgow	
1952	Aberdeen	
1953	Saltcoats	
1954	Inverness	
1955	Arbroath	
1956	Dumfries	Major-General SIR AYMER MAXWELL, C.B.E., M.C., D.L.
1957	St. Andrews	
1958	Edinburgh	
1959	Aberdeen	Mr T. MATHESON, O.B.E., J.P.

97

APPENDIX D

SUCCESSION LISTS

(a) **Presidents**
1921-1927. Field-Marshal EARL HAIG OF BEMERSYDE, K.T., G.C.B., O.M., G.C.V.O., K.C.I.E.
1927-1931. Admiral of the Fleet EARL JELLICOE, G.C.B., O.M., G.C.V.O.
1931-1947. General SIR IAN HAMILTON, G.C.B., G.C.M.G., D.S.O.
1947- . General SIR T. S. RIDDELL-WEBSTER, G.C.B., D.S.O., D.L.

(b) **National Chairmen**
1921-1922. SIR WILLIAM DICK-CUNYNGHAM, Bart.
1922-1923. Mr ANDREW YOUNG, J.P., F.E.I.S.
1923-1924. Captain J. L. CUMMING.
1924-1928. THE LORD GLENTANAR, D.L.
1929-1934. Captain THE EARL OF HADDINGTON, M.C.
1935-1946. Lieut.-Colonel THE EARL OF AIRLIE, K.T., G.C.V.O., M.C.
(During Lord Airlie's absence on Active Service, Colonel W. MARTIN KAY, C.M.G., C.B.E., T.D., D.L., National Vice-Chairman, carried on in his place.)
1946-1954. Major-General SIR JAMES SYME DREW, K.B.E., C.B., D.S.O., M.C., D.L.
1954-1958. Major-General SIR AYMER MAXWELL, C.B.E., M.C., D.L.
1958- . Mr T. MATHESON, O.B.E., J.P.

(c) **General Secretaries**
(1) 1919-1928. Mr HENRY BAXTER.
(2) 1928-1929. Commander P. F. NEWCOMBE, R.N.(Retd.)
(2A) Interim General Secretary, Mr GEORGE JOHNSTONE, M.B.E.
(3) 1929-1936. Lieut.-Colonel D. MATHERS, D.S.O., O.B.E., D.C.M.
(4) 1936-October 1945. Colonel J. M. B. SCOTT, O.B.E., T.D.
(4A) Interim General Secretary, Major WM. HENDRY, M.A.
(5) 1946- . Colonel C. S. MacLEOD OF GLENDALE, T.D.

WOMEN'S SECTION

Note.—From 1924 to 1939 the late COUNTESS HAIG OF BEMERSYDE was Patroness.

(a) **Presidents**
1924-1926. THE DUCHESS OF ATHOLL.
1926- . THE COUNTESS OF HADDINGTON.

(b) **Chairmen**
1924. Mrs McLEAN.
1924-1928. Mrs M. THOMSON.
1928-1935. Mrs S. CAMERON.
1935-1946. Mrs M. MacNEILL.
1946-1949. Mrs C. FAIRLEY, M.B.E.
1949-1953. Mrs C. K. MOIR.
1953-1956. Mrs M. G. ANDERSON.
1956-1959. Mrs A. B. R. STANLEY.
1959- . Mrs C. RORIE, B.E.M.

(c) **General Secretaries & Treasurers**
1924. Mrs CAMPBELL.
1924-1952. Mr G. JOHNSTONE, M.B.E
1952- . Mrs J. B. MORTON.

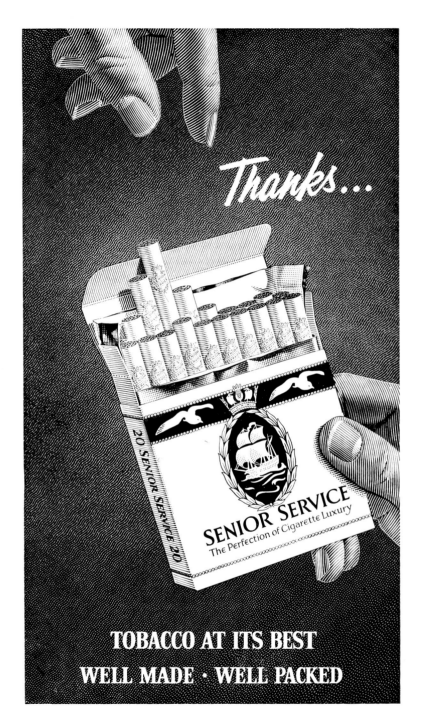

Thanks...

SENIOR SERVICE
The Perfection of Cigarette Luxury

20 SENIOR SERVICE 20

TOBACCO AT ITS BEST
WELL MADE · WELL PACKED

APPENDIX E

TABLE OF AREAS, AREA CHAIRMEN, BRANCHES AND WOMEN'S SECTION BRANCHES

Short Title.	Area Covered.	Area Chairman.
ABERDEEN . .	Aberdeenshire, Banffshire and Kincardineshire.	Mr A. Thomson, Lumphanan.
ANGUS AND PERTH-SHIRE.	Angus and Perthshire.	Mr Norman H. Barron, Montrose.
AYRSHIRE . .	Ayrshire.	Mr J. H. Stewart, Stewarton.
BORDERS . . .	Peeblesshire, Selkirkshire, Roxburghshire and Berwickshire.	Colonel D. McCorquodale, O.B.E., Kelso.
DUMFRIES AND GALLOWAY.	Dumfriesshire, Kirkcudbrightshire and Wigtownshire.	Mr John Ross, Lockerbie.
EDINBURGH AND LOTHIANS.	Edinburgh and the Lothians	Mr A. S. Stuart, M.B.E., Edinburgh.
FIFE AND KINROSS .	Fife and Kinross-shire.	Mr Norman R. King, St. Andrews.
GLASGOW AND WESTERN COUNTIES.	Renfrewshire, Dunbartonshire, Lanarkshire, Argyll, Stirlingshire and Clackmannanshire.	Mr M. M. Wilkie, Uddingston.
HIGHLANDS AND ISLANDS.	Inverness - shire, Ross-shire, Caithness, Nairnshire, Morayshire, Sutherland and Outer Isles.	Major John Mitchell, C.B.E., T.D., Inverness.

DATES OF FORMATION OF BRANCHES

* Denotes Women's Section Branch also formed. (See also end of Appendix for list of Women's Section Branches where there does not happen to be a similarly named Legion Branch.)

† Denotes possession of Colours.

Where there are two dates, the former usually refers to the fact that an ex-Serviceman's branch (e.g. Comrades of the Great War) was formed earlier and later merged into the Legion—or a Branch was resuscitated at a later date.

ABERDEEN

†Aberchirder .	.	.	.	1946	Dufftown and District	.	.	
*†Aberdeen	.	.	.	1921	†Ellon . . .	.	.	1928
†Aberlour, Craigellachie and District	.	.	.	1938	*†Fraserburgh .	.	.	1932
					†Fyvie . .	.	.	1948
†Aboyne .	.	.	.	1929	Glass . .	.	.	
†Alford .	.	.	.	1937	Grange. .	.	.	
*†Ballater and District	.	.	1926	Insch and District .	.	.	
†Banchory	.	.	.	1925	Inverbervie .	.	.	1926
Braemar	.	.	.	1932	*†Inverurie	.	.	1926
Buckie and District	.	.	1928	†Keith and District.	.	.	1936
†Bucksburn	.	.	.	1936	Kemnay .	.	.	
Cullen .	.	.	.	1926	†Kincardine O'Neil .	.	.	1926
Drummuir	.	.	.	1949	Kintore and District	.	.	1939

This is to Certify that

General Dwight D. Eisenhower

was unanimously elected to

Honorary Life Membership of

The British Legion (Scotland)

at its Annual Conference held in Edinburgh on Saturday the Twenty-sixth day of June, Nineteen hundred and Forty-three, in recognition of his indomitable and inspiring leadership as Commander-in-Chief of the Armed Forces of the United Nations in North Africa.

Signed for and on behalf of the British Legion (Scotland) this first day of October Nineteen hundred and Forty-three.

Ian Hamilton Gen¹ PRESIDENT.

CHAIRMAN.

GENERAL SECRETARY.

†Longside	. . . .	1922
†Lumphanan .	. . .	1950
Lumsden and District	. .	1958
Macduff	. . . .	{ 1946
		{ 1956
Maud .	. . . .	1948
†Methlick	. . .	1948
†Monquhitter .	. . .	
†New Pitsligo .	. . .	1946
*†Oldmachar .	. . .	1945
†Old Meldrum	. . .	1930
†Peterhead	. . . .	1926

Pitmedden	. . . .	1933
†Portsoy	. . . .	1937
Premnay	. . . .	
†Rhynie and District	. .	1930
*†Skene and Dunecht	. .	1928
Strichen	. . . .	
†Stuartfield	. . . .	1926
*†Tarves and District	. .	1947
Tomintoul and Glenlivet	.	1946
Torphins	. . . .	
Turriff and District	. .	
Upper Donside	. . .	

ANGUS AND PERTHSHIRE

*†Aberfeldy	. . . .	1930
*†Alyth .	. . . .	1922
†Arbroath	. . . .	1935
Auchterarder	. . .	1927
†Blair Atholl and Struan .		1931
†Blairgowrie .	. . .	1926
Braco and Greenloaning	.	1927
*†Brechin and District	. .	1928
Broughty Ferry	. . .	1944
†Callander	. . . .	{ 1919
		{ 1921
†Carnoustie .	. . .	
†Comrie	. . . .	1929
*†Coupar Angus	. . .	1939
*†Crieff .	. . . .	1930
†Doune and District	. .	1926
*†Dundee	. . . .	1921

†Dunkeld and Birnam	. .	1950
Fern .	. . . .	1949
†Ferryden	. . . .	{ 1919
		{ 1921
*†Forfar .	. . . .	1922
†Friockheim .	. . .	1936
Kinloch Rannoch .	. .	1930
*Kirriemuir .	. . .	1926
Mid Atholl .	. . .	1929
†Monifieth	. . . .	1944
†Montrose	. . . .	1931
†Muthill .	. . . .	1929
†Newtyle and District	. .	1937
*†Perth .	. . . .	1937
†Pitlochry	. . . .	1926
Tannadice and Oathlaw .	.	1921

AYRSHIRE

†Annbank, Mossblown, Drumley		1944
*†Ardrossan .	. . .	1926
†Auchinleck .	. . .	1934
*†Ayr .	. . . .	1928
*†Beith .	. . . .	1928
†Benwhat	. . . .	1935
*Brodick and Arran	. .	1929
†Catrine and Sorn .	. .	1944
*†Crosshill .	. . .	1948
*†Cumnock and District	. .	1926
*†Dailly and District	. .	1943
*†Dalry .	. . . .	1920
†Darvel .	. . . .	1920
Dunlop .	. . . .	
Fairlie .	. . . .	
†Galston	. . . .	1920
*†Girvan .	. . . .	1920
*†Irvine .	. . . .	1926
Kilmarnock .	. . .	1920
†Kilwinning .	. . .	1926

Lamlash, Whiting Bay and		
Southend .	. . .	1931
*†Largs .	. . . .	1926
†Mauchline	. . . .	1929
*Maybole	. . . .	1920
*†Monkton	. . . .	1945
†Muirkirk	. . . .	1944
*†New Cumnock	. . .	1936
*†Newmilns	. . . .	1935
†Ochiltree	. . . .	1930
*†Saltcoats	. . . .	1936
*†Stair .	. . . .	1930
*†Stevenston	. . . .	1929
†Stewarton	. . . .	1929
Stinchar Valley	. . .	1949
Straiton and Kirkmichael	.	1936
†Tarbolton	. . . .	1920
†Troon .	. . . .	1926
†West Kilbride	. . .	1926

DAKS REGD for days in the country

The art of a casual suit? Un-casual tailoring!

The advantage of a Daks casual suit is that it is extremely versatile. Comfort personified, it is tailored with such consummate skill that you can wear it not only in the country but in town.

Choose it in country worsted, or in the new Thorncroft, specially created for this type of suit. This beautiful cloth is lighter than ordinary thornproof, finer, softer and wonderful to wear.

BORDERS

Caddonfoot	1927
Chirnside	{ 1926 { 1948
†Coldstream	1926
Denholm	1926
*†Duns	1926
*Earlston	1926
Ettrick Forest . . .	1948
*Eyemouth	1927
*†Galashiels	{ 1926 { 1948
Galawater	1958
Gordon	{ 1929 { 1954

*†Hawick	1938
*†Innerleithen	{ 1926 { 1955
*†Jedburgh	1926
*†Kelso	1926
Lauderdale	{ 1927 { 1958
†Liddesdale	1947
†Lower Teviotdale . . .	1948
†Melrose	1926
*†Peebles	1926
†St. Boswells	1926
*†Selkirk	1926
†Upper Tweed . . .	1927

DUMFRIES AND GALLOWAY

†Annan	1928
Canonbie . . .	{ 1919 { 1921
†Castle Douglas . . .	{ 1919 { 1921
Creetown	1957
*†Dalbeattie and District .	1931
†Dumfries and Maxwelltown .	{ 1919 { 1921
Garlieston	1931
†Gatehouse of Fleet . .	1933
†Glencairn and Tynron . .	1921
Glenkens	
*†Glenluce	{ 1928 { 1948
Isle of Whithorn . . .	
†Kirkconnel	1937
Kirkcowan	1929
†Kirkcudbright . . .	{ 1919 { 1921

Kirkinner	
*†Langholm	1930
Lochmaben	1926
*†Locherbie	{ 1918 { 1921
*Moffat and District . .	1945
Mossdale and Laurieston .	1947
New Galloway and Kells .	1921
†Newton Stewart . . .	1928
*Port William	1928
*†Sanquhar	1936
Stoneykirk	1950
*†Stranraer	1928
†Thornhill and District . .	1935
Wamphray and Johnstone .	{ 1920 { 1921
Wanlockhead . . .	1932
Wigtown	1946

EDINBURGH AND LOTHIANS

*†Armadale	1931
*†Bathgate	1927
*†Bonnyrigg	1926
*†Broxburn	1930
Cockenzie and Port Seton .	1956
†Colinton	1928
†Corstorphine	1926
†Currie, Balerno and District .	1946
*†Dalkeith	1922
†Davidson's Mains, Blackhall and Cramond . . .	
Dirleton	1948
†Dryden	1948
*†Dunbar and District . .	1927
*†East Linton	1947
*†Edinburgh Eastern . .	1926

†Edinburgh Headquarters .	1927
†Edinburgh Jewish . . .	1931
*†Edinburgh Northern . .	1931
*†Edinburgh Western . .	1926
Gifford	1950
†Gullane	1929
*†Haddington	1936
†Juniper Green . . .	
Linburn	1951
*†Loanhead	1926
*†Longniddry	1941
*†Musselburgh	1927
†Newbattle and Gorebridge .	1955
*†North Berwick . . .	1926
*†Penicuik	1932

The Minister of Pensions and National Insurance, Mr John Boyd-Carpenter, M.P., with (*left*) the National President, General Riddell-Webster, and the new National Chairman, Mr Tom Matheson, chatting before the 1958 Conference held in Edinburgh. (From *The Claymore*, July 1958.)

Admiration of a Soldier. Statue to Field-Marshal Earl Haig of Bemersyde on the Esplanade of Edinburgh Castle. (From *The Claymore*, June 1958.)

Polton .	. . . .	1953
*†Portobello	. . .	1927
*Prestonpans .	. . .	1936
*†Roslin .	. . . .	1926
*†South Queensferry.	. .	1929
†Stoneyburn .	. . .	1931
*†Tranent	. . . .	
*†Uphall .	. . . .	1926
*West Calder .	. . .	1926
†West Linton .	. . .	
*†Whitburn	. . . .	1946
*†Winchburgh .	. . .	1931

FIFE AND KINROSS

Aberdour	. . . .	1932
*†Anstruther .	. . .	1930
*Auchtermuchty	. . .	1931
*Buckhaven .	. . .	1931
†Burntisland .	. . .	1926
†Ceres and District .	. .	1932
Coaltown-of-Wemyss	. .	
*Cowdenbeath	. . .	1928
*Crail .	. . . .	1932
*Crossgates	. . .	1948
†Cupar .	. . . .	1926
Dollar .	. . . .	1932
†Dunfermline .	. . .	1926
†East Wemyss	. . .	1928
*Elie and District	. . .	1931
Falkland	. . . .	1929
Freuchie	. . . .	
†Glenrothes	. . . .	1954
*Kelty and District.	. .	1933
†Kennoway .	. . .	1950
†Kincardine on Forth	. .	1932
Kinglassie	. . . .	1934
Kingskettle .	. . .	1931
†Kinross	. . . .	1931
*†Kirkcaldy .	. . .	1926
Ladybank	. . . .	1958
†Leuchars	. . . .	1928
*†Leven and District	. .	1926
*Lochore	. . . .	1926
*†Markinch .	. . .	1929
*Methilhill	. . . .	1947
Milnathort .	. . .	1926
*†Newburgh and District	.	1931
*Pittenweem .	. . .	1938
*Rosyth.	. . . .	1926
*†St. Andrews .	. . .	1932
*Tayport	. . . .	1934
Thornton	. . . .	1931
Windygates .	. . .	1931

GLASGOW AND WESTERN COUNTIES

Airdrie.	. . . .	1927
†Alloa .	. . . .	1926
†Alva and Menstrie.	. .	1937
Ardgowan	. . . .	1954
Ardrishaig and District .	.	1930
Baillieston	. . . .	1931
†Bannockburn	. . .	1934
Barrhead	. . . .	1946
Bearsden	. . . .	1946
†Bellshill	. . . .	1928
Benderloch .	. . .	1939
†Biggar and District	. .	1934
†Bishopbriggs.	. . .	1943
*Bonnybridge.	. . .	(1927 (1946
Bowmore	. . . .	1958
†Bridge of Allan	. . .	1921
†Bridge of Weir	. . .	1921
†Budhill and Springboig .	.	1929
†Burnside and District	. .	1944
†Cardonald	. . . .	1948
Cardross	. . . .	1949
Carluke	. . . .	1925
†Carmunnock .	. . .	1930
Carradale	. . . .	1945
Cenco .	. . . .	
Cleland.	. . . .	1942
*†Clydebank	. . . .	1921
†Coatbridge	. . . .	1921
*†Denny and District	. .	1936
*†Douglas and District	. .	1937
*Dumbarton .	. . .	1930
*Dunoon	. . . .	1921
†Drumchapel .	. . .	1946
Easdale	. . . .	1926
*†East Kilbride Parish	. .	1930
*†Falkirk.	. . . .	1943
†Forth .	. . . .	1946
*†Gargunnock .	. . .	1948
†Garrowhill .	. . .	1945
Gartcosh	. . . .	1927
Gartmore	. . . .	1921
†Giffnock and District	. .	1936
*†Glasgow Central .	. .	1921
†Glasgow Headquarters	. .	1926
†Glasgow Jewish	. . .	1928
*†Grangemouth	. . .	1936
*†Greenock .	. . .	1928
†Hamilton .	. . .	1921
†Helensburgh .	. . .	1935

On
National Service

REGISTERED
TRADE MARK

ELECTRIC—SOLID FUEL,

STEAM—OIL—GAS

CATERING EQUIPMENT,

DOMESTIC HEATING AND

COOKING APPLIANCES,

BATHS AND

SANITARY FITTINGS,

GENERAL CASTINGS

by

Telephone
FALKIRK 1100

ALLIED IRONFOUNDERS LTD.
FALKIRK   STIRLINGSHIRE

†Hutchesontown . . .	1933
Innellan and Toward . .	1933
†Johnstone	1925
	1935
Kilbarchan	1931
Kilfinan Parish . . .	1936
Kilmeny	1948
Killearn	1921
†Kilmun and District . .	1928
†Kilsyth and District . .	1936
†Kingspark and District . .	1943
Kippen	1936
Kirkfieldbank . . .	1950
†Kirkintilloch	1921
†Knightswood and District .	1944
†Lanark and District . .	1929
†Langside	1947
*†Larbert and District . .	1939
†Laurieston	1945
Lesmahagow	1929
Lochgoilhead . . .	1929
*Millport	1939
†Milngavie	1926
†Motherwell	1926
*†Neilston	1939
Newarthill	1937
Newton Mearns . . .	1946

North Motherwell . . .	1958
*Oban	1934
Old Kilpatrick . . .	1927
†Paisley Comrades . . .	1926
*†Polmont and District . .	1926
Port Ellen	1958
†Port Glasgow . . .	1932
*†Rothesay	1926
Rutherglen	1942
Sandbank	1946
†Shawlands	1921
	1953
*Shettleston and District .	1928
*†Shotts	1931
†Stirling	1926
Stonehouse	1929
Strachur and District . .	1949
Strathaven	1931
Strathblane	1955
Tarbert	1949
†Tillicoultry	1928
Tobermory	1924
Uddingston	1948
Upper Clyde	1946
Whitevale and Dennistoun .	1929
*†Wishaw	1926

HIGHLANDS AND ISLANDS

*Archieston	1949
*†Ardersier	1947
Assynt	
*Aviemore and Rothiemurchus .	1930
Avoch	1929
	1946
†Beauly	1947
Bettyhill	1948
Brora	1937
†Creich and Kincardine . .	1946
Cromarty	
*Dingwall	1933
†Dornoch	1937
Durness	1938
*Elgin and District . . .	1937
*†Forres	1919
	1951
Fort Augustus . . .	1927
	1946
†Fortrose and Rosemarkie .	1937
Fort William	1929
Glencoe and Ballachulish .	1934
Glengarry	
†Glenurquhart . . .	1948
Golspie	1926
†Halkirk and District . .	1947

*Helmsdale	1937
	1943
Hilton, Balintore and Shand-	
wick	1946
*†Invergordon	1935
*†Inverness	1921
†Kingussie	1926
Kinlochbervie . . .	1932
Kinlochleven	
Kintail and Glenshiel . .	1933
Kirkwall	1932
Lairg	1928
Latheron	1920
	1926
†Lerwick	1925
Lewis	1935
†Lochalsh	1949
†Lochbroom	1939
Lochcarron	
Longhope	1948
*Lossiemouth	
Mallaig	
Melness	
Muir of Ord	
†Nairn	1936
Newtonmore	1929

North Harris.	. . .	
North Mavine	. . .	1948
†North Skye .	. . .	(1932
		(1949
North Uist .	. . .	1928
Orphir and District	. .	
Rogart .	. . .	1955
Rothes .	. . .	
Sanday .	. . .	1946
Sandwick and District	.	1938
Scourie .	. . .	1952
Skerray Tongue	. .	1948
South Harris .	. . .	

South Ronaldsay and Burray .		
South Skye .	. . .	
South Uist .	. . .	
†Strathpeffer .	. .	(1925
		(1932
Strathspey .	. . .	1932
Stromness	. . .	
Tain .	. . .	1947
Thurso .	. . .	
Unst .	. . .	
Wall and District .	. .	
Wick .	. . .	1928
Yell .	. . .	1933

WOMEN'S SECTION BRANCHES IN EXISTING DISTRICTS WHERE THERE DOES NOT HAPPEN TO BE A SIMILARLY NAMED LEGION BRANCH

ANGUS AND PERTHSHIRE AREA

Dundee West.

EDINBURGH AND LOTHIANS AREA

Craigmillar.
Edinburgh Central.
Edinburgh South Side.
Fauldhouse.
Kirkliston.
Leith.

Livingston.
Lochend.
Newtongrange.
Prestonfield.
Slateford and Longstone.
Southfield.

FIFE AND KINROSS AREA

Blairadam.
Bowhill.
Leslie.

Lochgelly.
Methil and District.

GLASGOW AND WEST COUNTIES AREA

Arrochar.
Govan.
Lambhill.

Possilpark.
Yoker.

From the heart of Scotland

The " General Accident " is essentially a
Scottish concern. Its roots are in Perth where
it was started in 1885, and that initially small
company has grown to be one of the largest
Insurance companies in the British Isles, with
offices and agencies throughout the world.

Perhaps the principal reason for this re-
markable growth is the Corporation's reputation
for

SERVICE THAT EXCELS

FIRE AND LIFE ASSURANCE CORPORATION LIMITED

General Buildings, Perth

APPENDIX F

AFFILIATED REGIMENTAL ASSOCIATIONS

The Argyll and Sutherland Highlanders' Regimental Association.
Ayrshire Yeomanry Welfare Fund.
The Black Watch Association.
5th/7th Batt. Gordon Highlanders' Old Comrades' Association.
6th/11th Batt. Highland Light Infantry Association.
The Glasgow Highlanders' Association.
The King's Own Scottish Borderers' Association.
The Lovat Scouts (Glasgow Branch) Association.
1st Lowland Field Ambulance Benevolent Association.
The Women's Royal Army Corps Association (Edinburgh Branch).
The Queen's Own Cameron Highlanders' Regimental Association.
The Royal Scots Fusiliers' Association.
The Royal Scots Greys' Association.
The Royal Artillery Club, Glasgow.
The Scots Guards' Association Club, Edinburgh.
The Seaforth Highlanders' Regimental Association.
The Glasgow District Scottish Horse Association.
The Scots Guards' Association (Glasgow Branch).
The Cameronians (Scottish Rifles) Association.

APPENDIX G

BRITISH LEGION SCOTLAND PUBLICATIONS

1928-1939. *Pro Patria—The British Legion Scotland Journal.* This was published under both these titles.

1947-1950. British Legion Scotland *News Bulletin.*

1948-1958. *The Scottish Legionary*—an Annual.

1950-   . *The Claymore, (monthly).*

The following are regular publications issued by Headquarters, which are brought up-to-date as necessary :—

(1) *The British Legion Scotland Handbook* (for use of Members).

(2) Leaflet " Facts Tell ! " (setting out in concise form our Aims, Objects, Achievements and Hopes).

(3) Membership Application Form. (This is on the reverse of the " Facts Tell ! " leaflet.)

(4) Pamphlet " Notes for Speakers." (An informative guide for those addressing Meetings or giving guidance to prospective Members.)

(5) *Annual Diary.*

(6) *Christmas Cards.*

The winning Rink of the Tarbolton Branch in the 1956-57 Competition for the W. T. R. Houldsworth Curling Trophy (Ayrshire Area). The rink was also runner-up in 1954/55 and 1957/58. (From *The Claymore*, June 1958.)

Photograph by courtesy of L. P. Stephen, Photographer, Turriff.

Preparing the 1957 Legion Stand for the sale of Lady Haig's Poppy Factory goods, a regular feature at every Turriff Agricultural Association's Annual Show. (From *The Claymore*, October 1957.)

BRITISH LEGION SCOTLAND
Pension Appeal Tribunal Cases for the Period
1946 to 1958

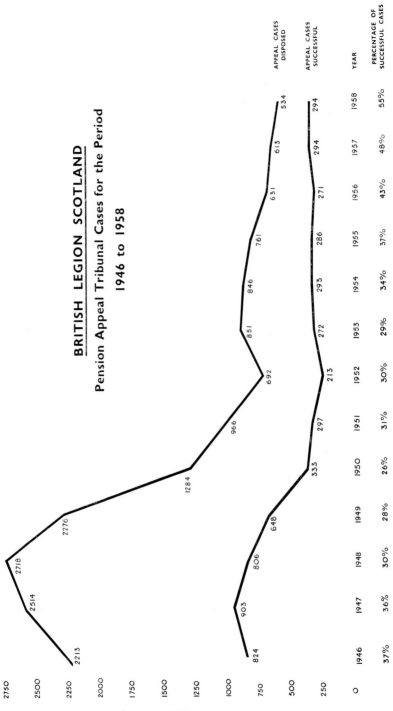

YEAR	1946	1947	1948	1949	1950	1951	1952	1953	1954	1955	1956	1957	1958
APPEAL CASES DISPOSED	824	903	2718	2276	1284	966	692	851	846	761	631	613	534
APPEAL CASES SUCCESSFUL			806	648	333	297	213	272	293	286	271	294	294
PERCENTAGE OF SUCCESSFUL CASES	37%	36%	30%	28%	26%	31%	30%	29%	34%	37%	43%	48%	55%

2213
2514

117

Sir Gerald Reece, K.C.M.G., Haddington Branch President, in happy mood amongst the winners in the 1956 Legion Gymkhana. (From *The Claymore*, October 1956.)

Photograph by courtesy of the " Galloway News."

The " top-table " at the British Legion Scotland Dumfries and Maxwelltown Branch's " Trench Supper." The tables had candles set in bottles to give the authentic atmosphere, and squibs were set off to imitate gunfire. (From *The Claymore*, June 1957.)

Photograph by courtesy of " Edinburgh Evening News."

Mr A. J. C. Provan, who fought in Gallipoli, lays the Wreath outside the National War Memorial, Edinburgh Castle, during the Anzac and Gallipoli Day Remembrance Service on 24th April 1954. (From *The Claymore,* June 1954.)

(Opposite)   *Photograph by courtesy of " The Scotsman."*

The Royal Review of the British Legion Scotland, held in King's Park, Edinburgh, in 1946. With the Royal Party are Colonel W. Robertson, V.C. (*left*) with Princess Elizabeth, the Earl of Airlie (*centre*) with His Majesty King George VI, and Major-General Sir James Drew (*right*) with H.M. The Queen.

Photograph by courtesy of James Hill (Photographers) Ltd., 38 Union Street, Greenock.

The Ardgowan Branch " Field of Remembrance " staged in tribute to the Unknown Soldier in Greenock Town Hall, 1955. (From *The Claymore*, November 1956.)

Courtesy of "Edinburgh Evening Dispatch."

Women's Section British Legion Scotland
PRESIDENT
THE COUNTESS OF HADDINGTON

(*Opposite*)   *Photograph by courtesy of " The Scotsman."*

The Royal Party on the platform at the Royal Review of the British Legion Scotland, held in King's Park, Edinburgh, in 1946. Conducting the Service is the Very Rev. Charles Warr, St. Giles' Cathedral and Dean of the Thistle.

A National Tradition

IT is a natural characteristic of the British to cling to their traditions—to the things they have proved worth while by the tests of time and use.

Since early this century the proprietors of 'Ovaltine' have established for this delicious food beverage a tradition of high quality and value which is outstanding. As a daytime beverage which helps to sustain and energize—as a nightcap which assists in promoting natural, restful sleep—'Ovaltine' stands in a class by itself. There is nothing like it.

1/6, 2/9 and 5/- per tin

Ovaltine
The World's most popular Food Beverage

P.882A

Photograph by courtesy of " The Scotsman."

General Sir Ian Hamilton, National President, pays his respects to Princess Elizabeth at the Royal Review of the British Legion Scotland, held in King's Park, Edinburgh, in 1946.

The Annual Conference of the British Legion Scotland, Inverness 1932. Sir Ian Hamilton on parade with H.R.H. The Prince of Wales (now Duke of Windsor). (From *The Claymore*, February 1951.)

H.R.H. smiles at the Ladies. Picture taken during the Inspection by H.R.H. The Duke of Edinburgh in King's Park, Edinburgh, on 28th June 1953. With His Royal Highness are (*l.* to *r.*) Mrs A. Stanley, Chairman, Edinburgh and Lothians Women's Section ; and Lieut.-Colonel The Hon. David Balfour, T.D., President, Edinburgh and Lothians Area and Parade Commander. His Royal Highness's Legion Badge and Tie will be noted. Salisbury Crags and Arthur's Seat can be seen towering in the background. (From *The Claymore*, August 1953.)

Photograph by courtesy of R. Clapperton of Selkirk.

The son of our Founder becomes engaged. Earl Haig walking in the grounds of Bemersyde with Miss Adrienne Thérèse Morley, on the announcement of their engagement. (From *The Claymore*, August 1956.)

The Royal Review, London, 1951. The Scottish contingent passes H.M. King George VI at the saluting base. Major-Gen. Sir James Drew, Chairman, is seen leading the Parade, followed by Col. Colin MacLeod of Glendale, General Secretary. (From *The Claymore*, June 1951.)

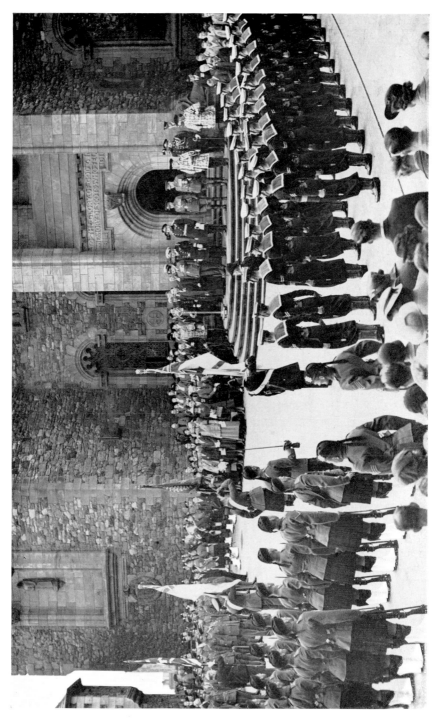

Photograph by courtesy of the " Border Standard."

The Standards at the 1953 Galashiels Festival of Remembrance Service which was addressed by the National Chairman. (From *The Claymore*, January 1954.)

(*Opposite*)   *Photograph by courtesy of " Scottish Pictorial Press, Edinburgh."*

" For the Fallen." The 1936 Parade at the National Shrine in Edinburgh Castle, with the Royal Navy Standard-Bearer in full dress. The Legion Standard-Bearer (*left*) is Captain J. Robb, M.M.

Photograph by courtesy of " Peeblesshire News."

A tribute to the fallen during the Service held at Peebles War Memorial during the 1958 Annual Conference of the Women's Section. (From *The Claymore*, August 1958.)

(*Opposite*)

" COLOURS ARE THE EMBLEMS OF LOYALTY AND DUTY "

The King's Colour (now the Queen's Colour) and the British Legion Scotland Standard. (From *The Claymore*, Conference Number, 1950.)

Staig.

The National President, British Legion Scotland, General Sir Thomas Riddell-Webster, receiving the Bronze Bust of himself presented by the Angus and Perth Area Council. L. to r.) Brigadier H. J. D. Clark, Provost Dr. D. Stewart and Lady Riddell-Webster. (From *The Claymore*, April 1957.)

(Opposite)

The representatives at the inaugural meeting of the Comrades of the Great War and the Scottish Federation of Ex-Servicemen to form the British Legion Scotland in 1921. The photograph was taken outside the premises of the West End Ex-Servicemen's Club in Edinburgh.

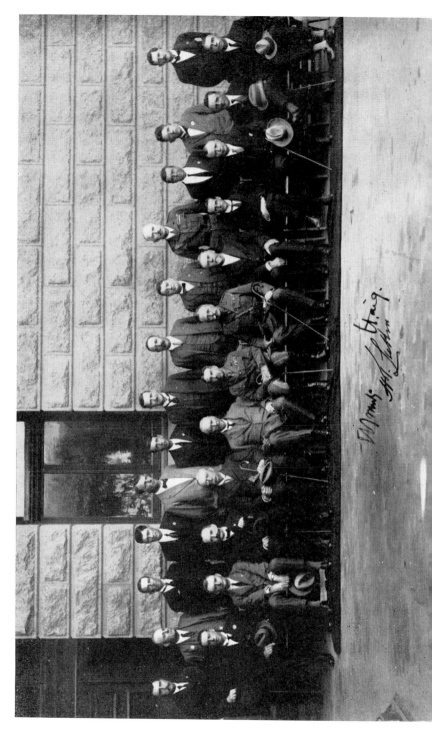

Photograph by courtesy of the " Perthshire Advertiser."

It is not often we get a photograph of the Navy, but here is one at last. This shows the smart turnout by members of the Girls' Nautical Training Corps in the 1956 Legion's Remembrance Day Parade at Perth. (From *The Claymore*, February 1957.)

(Opposite)   *Photograph by courtesy of Edgcome & Co., Cape Town.*

The first Conference of " The British Empire Service League," City Hall, Cape Town, 28th February to 4th March 1921 of Representatives of Ex-Servicemen's Organisations within the British Empire. (From *The Claymore*, January 1958.)

Photograph by courtesy of Mr Kenneth McEwan, Glasgow.

Culzean (taken from an oil painting by J. D. Clark in the possession of Captain J. Robb).
To this castle General Dwight D. Eisenhower, Commander-in-Chief of the Allied Forces in
Europe during World War II, has the right of entry to apartments therein, gifted to him
by the Scottish people, to take up residence whenever he wishes.

The Accordionist amuses Lady Wheatley at the Southfield Women's Section 5th Anniversary Party in 1955. (From *The Claymore*, January 1956.)

Photograph by courtesy of Norwood Inglis, Edinburgh.

Our War-Blinded Comrades prove their energetic strength at Linburn. (From *The Claymore*, April 1953.)

Photograph by courtesy of " Dundee Courier and Advertiser."

Building for the future.   Volunteers at work on the Branch's new Hall at Forfar.   (From *The Claymore*, February 1955.)

Photograph by courtesy of " Edinburgh Evening News."

At the " Presentation Day " Ball organised on behalf of National Funds and held in the Assembly Rooms, Edinburgh, on 3rd July 1958. (*L. to r.*) Major-General Sir Aymer Maxwell, Lady Haig (Chairman of the Ball), Captain Douglas Morton (Ball Secretary) and Lord Haig. (From *The Claymore*, September 1958.)

The Company assembled at the Inverurie and District Branch New Year Party when Mr T. Bisset (*fourth from left*) was presented with a replica of the Cup he won at the 1958 Standard-Bearing Competition, Edinburgh. (From *The Claymore*, March 1959.)

Courtesy of Mr G. F. Ford, The Studio, Cupar, Fife.

The Legion's Floodlit Garden of Remembrance at St. John's Church, Cupar, in 1956. From *The Claymore*, February 1957.

Mr L. G. Durward, Chairman, Banchory Branch, presenting a cheque to Private Donald Davidson, Champion Recruit, The Gordon Highlanders Depot. (From *The Claymore*, April 1956.)

Photograph by courtesy of Norwood Inglis, 18 Regent Terrace, Edinburgh.

"Congratulations, old boy—she's all yours." The National Chairman, Major-General Aymer Maxwell, hands over the First Prize in the 1956 Competition of Skill on the Derby, in aid of National Funds, to Mr Donald MacPherson of Dollar. (From *The Claymore*, July 1956.)

Photograph by courtesy of James Weir, 29 Westburn Street, Greenock.

A happy band of Cricketers at the Legion *v.* Greenock Match at Adrgowan, in 1955. (From *The Claymore*, July 1955.)

The 1956 Remembrance Day Parade of the South Queensferry Branch, headed by the 67th Boys' Brigade (Edinburgh Company) Pipe Band. Over 400 turned out—the biggest Parade ever held. (From *The Claymore*, March 1957.)

Photograph by courtesy of " Edinburgh Evening News."

Major W. Peters, U.S.A.F., laid a wreath on the Scottish-American War Memorial in Princes Street Gardens, Edinburgh, during the 1955 Commemoration Service. A wreath was laid by Mr Alex. Stuart for the British Legion Scotland. (From *The Claymore*, September 1955.)

Photograph by courtesy of Bewsy, 3 Murray Street, Annan.

The Pipe Bands entered for the Annan Championship during the Riding of the Marches celebrations on 5th July 1958, and won by the Annan British Legion Pipe Band. (From *The Claymore*, September 1958.)

Courtesy of "The Bulletin," Glasgow

At the "presentation parade" of the
Standard Car which was the first prize in
the Competition of Skill on the Derby
young Robert Wedderburn, elder son of
Major T. M. Wedderburn, Hon. Legal
Adviser to the British Legion Scotland, is
seen presenting Miss Vivien Leigh with a
bouquet. Looking smilingly on is Marshal
of the Royal Air Force, Lord Tedder
Chairman of Standard Motors. (From *The
Claymore*, June 1956.)

A happy group. Johnstone Branch, British Legion Scotland, Physical Training Class
for Youths. (From *The Claymore*, July 1954.)

Photograph by courtesy of " The Bulletin."

he Countess of Dalkeith who opened the 1958 Mannequin Parade in Edinburgh, in aid
f National Funds, is seen in conversation with Captain Gordon Greensmith Downes
ate London Scottish and Gordon Highlanders) the sponsor of ten parades for our funds.
(From *The Claymore*, May 1958.)

Photograph by courtesy of " Kilmarnock Standard."

he Standards at the 1955 Re-dedication Service of the Galston Branch. (From *The
Claymore*, July 1955.)

A smiling group at the Giffnock and District Branch's outing to Troon in 1958 of th
fatherless children. (From *The Claymore*, August 1958.)

Photograph by courtesy of " Hawick News.

Field-Marshal Lord Harding (*third from left*) who was guest speaker at the British Legio
Scotland, Hawick Branch Dinner in 1959. (From *The Claymore*, February 1959.)

Photograph by courtesy of " Edinburgh Evening News.

Chief Guests at the Edinburgh Jewish Branch Dinner. (*L. to r.*) Mr B. Lewis (*Chairman*
Sir James Ferguson, Mr R. Cohen, Hon. Life President, Sheriff R. N. Levitt and Lieut
Colonel The Hon. D. A. Balfour. (From *The Claymore*, February 1958.)

Lord Haig laying a Commemoration Wreath at the foot of the Plaque of his father, Field-Marshall Earl Haig, in the National Shrine in Edinburgh Castle. (From *The Claymore*, April 1952.)

Photograph by courtesy of " Bon Accord," Aberdeen.

Pictured with their Hostesses are some of the fifty Old Age Pensioners who attended a Party given for them by the Oldmachar Women's Section. (From *The Claymore*, April 1959.)

The late Major-General Sir James Symes Drew, K.B.E., C.B., D.S.O., M.C., D.L., for seven years Chairman, British Legion Scotland. The portrait is by Sir William Hutchison, P.R.S.A., HON. R.A., and was presented by the Legion to Sir James at the Annual Conference in Inverness in 1954. (From *The Claymore*, August 1954.)

Photograph by courtesy of " The Scotsman."

Our photograph shows H.M. The Queen inspecting the V.C. Parade in Hyde Park.
Colonel Findlay's commanding figure will be noticed as right marker. He was a member
of the National Executive Council. (From *The Claymore*, September 1956.)

Photograph by courtesy of " Picture Illustrations," London.

Sir Ian Hamilton's Legion activities were not confined to the north of the Border.
He is shown here, on the left of the platform, with Field-Marshal Lord Milne at a
British Legion Cenotaph Parade in 1940. The contingent seen on Horseguards Parade
is from Winchester.

The Guiser-Jarl's Squad and the Galley during the 1955 " Up Helly A " Celebrations a Lerwick, Scotland.   (From *The Claymore*, January 1956.)

" The Masque of Scotland," produced in aid of national funds in Glasgow in 1950. The picture shows " Mary Queen of Scots " and her ladies. (From *The Claymore*, November 1950.)